Dinner, DONE!

40 Healthy Recipes + 5 Kitchen Tools to Put
Menu Planning on Auto-Pilot and
Always Have an Answer to
"What's for dinner?"

Jen Haugen, RDN, LD

GET YOUR FREE GIFT!

Before you dive into this book, my gift to you is the Dinner, Done! Planner. It includes my printable 6-week Dinner, Done! menu plan with essential pantry, refrigerator, and freezer ingredients, plus kitchen organization tips and tools recommended for speedy meal preparation.

If you don't have a copy, then grab it for FREE right here: www.jenhaugen.com/dinnerdone

I dedicate this book to my two kids, for whom I have always loved cooking. Our meals are always better when the two of you are at the table sharing your stories and smiles.

Thank you to my true love, my husband, who continually eats whatever I make, but isn't afraid to share his honest opinion. Looking across the table at you has always been my favorite and I love how you take your hat off when it's time to eat.

TABLE OF CONTENTS

Introduction xi

I. MEAL PLANNING MOM 3

II. MOM'S FOREVER DINNER PLAN 15

Kitchen Quiz
Quick Kitchen Audit
Top Kitchen Tools to Make Meals Easier
Essential Meal Planning Strategy
Recipe List

III. PRESSURE COOKER RECIPES 33

Chicken & Wild Rice Soup
Broccoli Cheese Soup
Hearty Minnesota Chili
Spaghetti
Fettuccine Alfredo with Chicken
Creamy Chicken Pesto Pasta
Egg Roll in a Bowl
Chicken Burrito Bowls
Beef Stew
Macaroni and Cheese
Simple Side Dish: Salad Mix & Match

IV. AIR FRYER RECIPES 51

Barbecue Sriracha Chicken Wings
Crispy Chicken Tenders
Crunchy Cod
Hawaiian Coconut Shrimp
Steak Kebabs
Rotisserie Pork Tenderloin
Pizza Stromboli
Simple Side Dish: Roasted Vegetables

V. GRILL/GRIDDLE RECIPES   67

Panini Night
Smashed Slider Bar Night
French Toast for Dinner
Quesadilla Night
Ginger Brown Sugar Glazed Salmon
Chicken Fajitas
Simple Side Dish: Smoothie Maker

VI. ONE POT RECIPES   81

Barbecues
General Tso Chicken and Vegetable Stir Fry
Chicken Pot Pie
Tater Tot Casserole
Zesty Pasta Skillet
California Chicken and Rice Casserole
Taco Bubble Casserole
Creamy Turkey and Noodles
Sheet Pan Dinners
Simple Side Dish: Snacking Vegetable Platter

VII. PIZZA RECIPES   97

Make Ahead Homemade Pizza Dough
5-Minute Homemade Pizza Dough
Barbecue Chicken Pizza
Healthy Hawaiian Pizza
Garden Fresh Pizza
Italian Sausage Pesto Pizza
Taco Pizza
Chicken Fajita Pizza
Detroit-Style Pizza
Thai Chicken Pizza
Simple Side Dish: Fresh Fruit and Dips

VIII. NEXT STEPS   115

TABLE OF CONTENTS

Sometimes you never know the value of a moment,

until it becomes a memory.

~Dr. Seuss

Introduction

"What's for dinner?" Everyday I get asked this question. Do you? And do you always have an answer? The struggle is real for many of us. And while we know eating out is expensive, and running through the drive-through only to pass out burgers behind the seat is guilt-inducing, meal planning to avoid eating out can be so tedious and boring. It takes too much time, and it's overwhelming to make decisions about what to cook when decision fatigue has set in after a long day. Scrolling for recipes that everyone will eat is a total time suck, and trying to create a menu just does not seem realistic on top of everything else on our plates, so eating out and buying convenience meals tend to win. But while they may put food in the belly in the short term, over the long term there can be negative effects on health. And when dinner has quite literally taken a back seat, the biggest loss I feel at that moment is the loss of family connection. No one is looking at each other across the table - but rather, we are mindlessly eating just to get to the next activity.

You may not always have the answer to that age-old question of "What's for dinner?". But with this book, I'm going to show you how to solve that dilemma. I'm going to give you my exact menu map to make your Forever Dinner Plan — a plan that you will use over and over again during your busiest season in life. It not only will save you oodles of money because you aren't spending your hard-earned cash at the drive-through, but it will also save you tons of time and your health too. I have developed a system for you to use every single week no matter how busy you are to help you create fast and healthy meals every night of the week. You will become a kitchen rockstar!

You will learn how to save the most time in the kitchen on your busiest night of the week with a kitchen tool that will change your dinner planning forever. I will teach you how to use an air fryer to make a healthy family meal in minutes that you can be proud to put on the table for your family. You will see how to replicate some of your family's favorite restaurant meals at home in a fraction of the time. You will get my best tip to eliminate all the extra clean up in the kitchen when the week has been too long. Last, but not least, I will provide you with the one thing I did with my family that brought us closer and led to deeper connections.

Most of all, I am going to teach you a system for menu planning that will allow you to always have the answer to "What's for dinner?" every night of the week without mindlessly searching for answers.

In 2001, I became a registered dietitian because of my passion for helping people improve their health with food and nutrition. I took classes on menu planning, wrote menus professionally, and built shopping lists for my clients. I taught my clients to shop for the right ingredients to make healthy meals at home, to create a menu plan that worked for their lifestyle, and to cook easy recipes that would align with their health goals.

In 2003, my son was born. I had high expectations for myself and wanted to make everything homemade — homemade baby food and homemade breakfast, lunch, and dinner. My goal was to have a menu plan for every meal, every day, and I had a lofty goal to never expose him to fast food. High hopes for a new mom.

This became a recipe for failure. I commuted two hours a day to my dietitian job. I left the house at 5:45 in the morning and didn't return until 5:45 at night. With this schedule, my elevated expectations dwindled quickly. By the time I had my daughter 21 months later, I was overwhelmed and disappointed with myself because I couldn't live up to the expectations I set for myself as a mom and as a dietitian. I tried all kinds of meal planning techniques in my own kitchen to help make things simpler, including the most archaic where I drew a calendar on a piece of paper and plotted recipes onto it after I spent hours perusing multiple cookbooks. I've also tried a more advanced form of meal planning by creating a cycle menu. I have scrolled and pinned and plotted recipes into menus digitally and then written out shopping lists. I simply found that while my intentions were good, the execution was inconsistent because it wasn't based on my schedule and lifestyle needs, and it wasn't based on the tools I had to prepare and cook my meals. I was improvising my way through dinner almost 100% of the time. Over 80% of us do not have a plan for dinner at 4:00 p.m., and I fit right into that. I was a dietitian who was supposed to be the expert in menu planning and having a healthy dinner on the table every night of the week. Instead I felt I was an epic failure (without anyone really knowing). Why couldn't I get it together at home?

But then everything changed when I was introduced to certain cooking tools that brought new life to my kitchen. These tools made me look like a pro, and they were fun to use. Soon I was cooking from-scratch dinners almost every night of the week, including coming up with my own recipes. Plus, I built a meal plan around these recipes to simplify everything. I was happier because I wasn't overloaded with drive-through guilt. I was proud of what I was serving — something healthy, balanced, and quick to prepare.

And the compliments started.

"Mom, thanks for making dinner, it was really good."

And at that moment in time, all seemed right with the world. I was less stressed, felt less guilt, and I felt empowered.

I can't wait to share my simple technique with you. I love teaching and helping others simplify and make things more efficient than they ever thought possible. I wrote this book for you so you don't have to come up with a plan for dinner alone. You don't have to have it all together (I certainly didn't). You don't have to spend hours meal planning like I have. Instead, I will be right by your side in the kitchen, guiding you to healthy family meals by using my Forever Dinner plan.

You are going to feel so much less stress once you implement the Forever Dinner Plan. It won't take long for you to see the impact. You'll have more money in your wallet, more time with your family, more joy and happiness in your life, and better health for everyone in your household. You may not think that a simple meal plan could do all that, but let me show you how.

For a long time, I never realized the impact my unorganized home meal planning was having on our family. Working late? Let's grab a bite to eat at the burger joint. In between activities? Let's pass through the sandwich shop. One month when the credit card bill came, we realized we had spent almost $1,000 on food. While some of that was food from the grocery store, a large chunk of it was eating out more than I would like to admit, including fast food and fast casual restaurants. That money could have gone towards other things that would have a longer-lasting impact, like college savings, retirement savings, and fun experiences we had always hoped to have. And with high blood pressure in my family history, along with cancer and heart disease, the extra ten pounds I gained were a wake up call.

I've had clients I work with share these same struggles, and when they realize the power of this simple way to meal plan, things change in big ways.

"I never learned how to plan dinner when I was growing up, and constantly felt like a failure when trying to cook for my family. Now I feel so empowered and

confident in the kitchen with this simple meal planning strategy. Plus I'm saving so much time, not just with cooking, but also with the scrolling and the pinning and the plotting out dinner I used to spend what felt like hours on!"

"Every time we go through the drive-through, it's over $30 for a family of four, and that was starting to happen several times a week. Instead, by following this plan, I am cooking at home every night of the week and saving more than $100 a week!"

"I'm a happier wife and mom because I am able to accomplish all that I wanted to do - make a healthy meal for my family to gather around the table so we can connect after a long day without even thinking about it because of this simple plan."

I can promise you that by reading this entire book, implementing the Forever Dinner Plan meal planning strategy, and using the recipes and kitchen tools I recommend, you not only will save quite a bit of money and oodles of time in the kitchen, but you will be able to do what you never thought was possible — never have to think about "What's for dinner?" again!

I once read that Steve Jobs had all the same clothes in his closet to eliminate the energy it took to make that seemingly small decision at the beginning of the day. I am doing the same for you. I am helping you eliminate decision fatigue and the overwhelming struggle with cooking a balanced meal for your family by being the mom dietitian who has empowered you and chosen the simple meals you can make for your family every night of the week.

Let's get you started on the Forever Dinner Plan immediately so you don't have to worry any more about how to create healthy meals for your family. Time is money. Don't spend the extra time plotting and planning. Instead, use my strategy today and you will feel so much better about being asked, "Mom, what's for dinner?"

CHAPTER ONE

Meal Planning Mom

*"Growing up, I learned a lot of life's lessons
at the dinner table."*

~Chef John Besh

I remember it like it was yesterday. I was watching my son, who was not yet one year old, crawl across the kitchen floor. I had music on in the background and a Kenny Chesney song, "There Goes My Life," came on. Tears started to run down my face because time was already going too fast.

Here was this little boy who I had given birth to just a few months prior, crawling away from me to explore something new that captured his attention. Even though I knew there were a lot of years ahead that would involve letting go, there was something about this moment that has stuck with me all this time. It felt in this brief moment that I could snap my fingers and he would be all grown up.

When my son graduated from high school and left one month later for his induction into the military, tears streamed down my face. I felt as if I had lost my purpose. Even though my daughter was still at home, things had changed in a big way and my momma's heart felt it. From a very young age, my answer to the "what do you want to be when you grow up" question was always "a mother." It didn't sound as glamorous as a doctor or lawyer or scientist, but it was what I wanted deep in my heart. Because somehow I knew that as a mom, I would be able to change the world through the love I shared with my family. And as I reflect, much of that love was shown through my cooking for them and all those dinner table dates we had as a family.

During my time as a supermarket dietitian, I taught hundreds of cooking classes for kids and families. I gave thousands of grocery store "healthy food" tours to help people make healthy choices on a daily basis. During that time, I realized that it was often the moms who held the power to change their families' eating habits for the better. This is because moms tend to spend a lot of time in the kitchen. Either by nature, by choice, or by circumstance, it generally just happens.

In our home, the kitchen has always been the heart of the household. I recently did the math to learn that during an eighteen year period, we would have eaten dinner at the table 6,570 times. That is astronomical, and it shows what a huge role that table plays in our daily life. Not only did eating happen at the table, but it's also where homework was completed. With those thousands of meals, we also had thousands of conversations about our school days and work days and thousands of questions asked and answered about values and friendships and life choices. We celebrated holidays in the kitchen with our favorite foods. We celebrated birthdays with a special breakfast or dinner on the "Special Day Plate". We celebrated daily and weekly wins including college admission letters, good scores on tests, and good decisions made. We shared hard stories and struggles, and good stories and good struggles. Without the kitchen, where would all these things take place?

If I took a survey of who is in charge of the kitchen at home, most would answer in most homes, it's mom. Moms tend to be in charge of the cooking, the prepping, the grocery shopping, the clean up, the dishwasher emptying, the dishwasher filling, and kitchen organizing. The selecting of recipes, the menu planning, the forethought of getting things out of the freezer to manage the busy week ahead and more. All of this sounds like a job description, and it's a lot if you think about it! The whole household relies on mom to keep the heartbeat of the home running. And moms do it without any pay.

When I first became a mother, I absolutely knew that I wanted to be the one who did all the things in the kitchen, especially because I was a registered dietitian. Thinking back to my childhood, it seemed natural for me to want to create everything from scratch, as I had loved being in the kitchen since I was a child. I think I taught myself a lot of reading skills just by reading old church cookbooks. As a teen, I was giving food and recipe demonstrations to my 4-H club members. Then, I went to college for dietetics and food and nutrition and got my degree. So naturally, after I had my first child, I thought I must make homemade baby food, make all meals from scratch, and never take my kids to a fast food restaurant.

Well, that didn't last long. By the time I had my daughter 21 months after my son, I was buying baby food, making meals the "semi-homemade" way with convenience foods that were definitely not as healthy, and we had made our way through the McDonalds drive-through for those beloved Happy Meals a few times. These habits were not making me happy though as a mom and dietitian. It was the complete opposite. I was feeling like I had failed my family and, maybe even more significant, failed myself. I thought I could do it all but it wasn't happening. Why? Because I was overwhelmed. I was working full-time, commuting two hours a day, and the most precious hour I had before my kids went to their early bedtime as little toddlers was the hour after I got home; I didn't want to spend that hour cooking. And while meal planning was on my radar on the weekend, I cherished the time to rejuvenate and play with my kids, and it just didn't get done.

So, instead, I started to gravitate towards the convenience foods we would find in the grocery store. Or we would go through the drive-through for supper in a sack as a way to minimize time in the kitchen so I could maximize time with my kids. I even put them to bed in the clothes they would wear the next day as a way to save time in the mornings, too. I knew I needed to use my skills as a dietitian to create a better routine, but time was getting in the way. I was meal planning for people in my professional dietitian life, and it didn't make sense as to why I couldn't do it for my personal life as well.

As my kids grew, things got busier and I took on even more roles. It was almost like a snowball effect. Having children made my life busy, of course, but when I was asked to be a part of something to help the school or church or do extra volunteer work, I had a hard time saying no.

One day, I was getting ready to back the car out of the garage for our monthly Parent Teacher Association meeting. I looked for my kids and they were nowhere to be found. I remember shifting my head in different directions and not seeing them anywhere. I started to panic. Everything felt as if it were slow motion. I was literally looking for the iconic "white van" without windows — a telltale sign that a stranger was holding them captive. I was going into full-on anxiety mode. But before I knew it, my new neighbor (who probably thought I was a crazy mom and I hadn't even officially met him yet), pointed towards the back of our backyard shed. And there they were.

It was at that moment I realized my life included too many things to do and not enough time with my family. Too many activities over the dinner hour. Too many meetings that I raised my hand for because I felt guilty not being involved. Too many nights of backseat supper-in-a-sack meals because we had to get to the next thing and my meal planning was suffering. It was at that moment that I decided it had to come to a halt. I had to stop saying yes to the wrong things so I could say yes to the right things.

So, I made a few changes for the better, including really focusing on being organized, eliminating the extra in the schedule, and using a whole new approach to meal planning in the kitchen. That's when I decided that my professional meal planning techniques needed to be applied at home.

What were those techniques? The one I wanted to implement right away was a cycle menu. If I could do that professionally, then why couldn't I do it at home? This type of meal planning basically puts together four weeks of meals and then you rotate through those same meals each month, on a cycle. It can be quite a lot of work on the front end, as you pull out the top twenty to twenty-five meals you love to eat and make, and then plot them into the rotation. This type of meal planning really helps with decision fatigue, and once you do it once, you can use it again and again, and even create a shopping list from it.

Then came a new challenge. My pretty menu plan wasn't always getting accomplished because of that same old reason: time. My kids had gotten older and were involved in sports and other activities, so we were back to the supper in a sack mentality again. Church meetings, work meetings, and other events were peeling away the dinner hour. These events would throw off my schedule, or the schedule would change on a whim and the next thing you know — that fancy meal plan just wasn't working any more.

What happened next became just the thing that I needed. As I was shopping online one day to look for a veggie spiralizer to help with boosting vegetables in our meals, I instead decided to become an independent consultant with Pampered Chef. I was intrigued by the way kitchen tools could help me streamline things in the kitchen and perhaps make cooking fun again. I started to use these new tools to prep meals faster than I ever thought possible. Cooking became faster as well because of the way the tools worked. At that point, I felt a new sense of freedom, all because of kitchen tools. Freedom to spend time with my kids again while dinner was cooking in the pressure cooker. Freedom to be flexible in meals in case the schedule shifted — hello air fryer that doesn't need to preheat like the oven.

Freedom to make meals I actually wanted to make because I had the right tools to help me make it happen.

My "aha" moment included this math equation: Menu planning + the right kitchen tools = the perfect combination of getting dinner done fast. This meant I could spend more time with my family doing things we enjoyed. It all made sense - I thought about how many times I was giving a "healthy foods grocery store tour" where, after the tour, my clients said, "Will you come to my house now and help me learn how to prepare these foods into recipes?" This was the magic bullet I had been looking for.

You may think kitchen tools couldn't seriously make that much of a difference, but there are many things about kitchen tools that can transform your cooking in the kitchen. Just like we don't cut the grass in the yard with a scissor (at least I hope you don't), we instead use a power tool that can speed up the time it takes to get the job done. But there had to be some criteria for these tools. The tools had to be:

- Fun and easy to use
- Made well so they last a long time
- Time-saving in major ways
- Leaving more money in my wallet (because of not eating out as much)
- Specifically allow for a "set it and forget it" cooking style (no babysitting the pot while you are trying to do a bunch of other things)
- Helping me cook fast and healthy meals that tasted great!

There are definitely tools that meet these criteria, but before we dive into those, I want to shed some light on frequently found myths about meal planning so you can move beyond them and start to take action to get your family life back!

Meal Planning Myths

1. Meal planning takes forever. I used to sit down on the weekends, pull out my cookbooks, look at our schedule, and try to plot and plan. That did take forever! Now, with the strategy you are going to learn in this book, I assign a tool to a day of the week based on our schedules and pick a recipe. It's so much simpler, and it saves time and money, too.

2. Meal planning isn't fun. It can be fun when the process is smooth. What isn't fun is when there isn't a process. I know many times my "process" was opening the freezer door and picking out a convenience meal, but that didn't always leave me feeling good about what I was putting on the table. So instead, this process is based on the tool of the day, and it matches our schedule, leaving a lot more room for creativity.

3. Cooking is a chore. This is a mindset issue. Instead of thinking of it as one more thing to do each day, think instead about how it nourishes both your family and your soul. Making something with our hands is just like creating a piece of art. When we put our heart and soul into cooking, no matter how short a time it takes, it's still homemade from the heart. I like to say that cooking is how we can show our love.

4. My family won't like the food I make — Why bother? I totally get it. A picky eater or two can change the dynamics of food preparation, making you think you have to make two separate meals. There are two things you can do: get your picky eater involved in the meal preparation, and put at least one thing on the menu they enjoy. They will learn to try new things when you give them a chance to try new things.

5. Eating healthy is too expensive. I've battled this one a lot over the years, including when I worked in the supermarket. It's much more inexpensive to eat healthy at home than it is to eat out. Some of the most inexpensive foods are actually healthy ones — think beans, bananas, whole grain rice, frozen fruits, and in season fruits and vegetables, just to name a few. And these foods can round out a meal with side dishes to boost the nutrition of any meal. You can make an impact on your budget by eating healthy meals at home.

Meal Planning Mindset

You may come from a background of convenience meals from a box or from the freezer. You may come from a background of the drive-through being the first choice for dinner. Old habits are hard to break. But I encourage you to start small and choose one night a week to incorporate this strategy so it fits your lifestyle, and you can cook one of the many meals featured in this book on that night. It could quite possibly change your life.

Instead, come to the kitchen with the mindset of "Making a fast and healthy meal is not only super nourishing to my family, but it also allows me to save money and give me more time with them."

Meal Planning Lessons Learned

- You CAN make a healthy meal in minutes. Despite what you may believe, cooking a healthy meal does not need to take all day. Most of the recipes in this book are meant to help you finish cooking in less than twenty-five minutes.
- Let the tools do the work. This is the part I see most people struggle with. When you say "I don't have time to cook," what I think you really mean is that you don't have the right tools to make cooking fast. I'm here to help you with that. I have a list of tools in the next chapter that will totally streamline your prep and cooking time.
- You can use a cycle menu with success at home too. If you really want to get things streamlined and make your kitchen so efficient it almost runs itself, then use the cycle menu I have prepared for you. You won't have to think about what's for dinner again. This comes from years of professional menu planning. Cycle menus are so worthwhile and efficient; that's why every professional food service organization uses them.
- It doesn't have to be complex. Making a meal that's healthy and balanced is not complex at all. In fact, a lot of it is about the side dishes you serve with the meal that provide the balance you are looking for. I have included ideas in each chapter to help you.

- It's fun to explore and get creative in the kitchen. While one of my pastimes is reading and looking at cookbooks, it may not be something you enjoy. But, when cooking becomes easy and simple, you tend to explore a little more with new recipes and new tools which inject creativity into your dinner life.
- Meal planning saves time and money. This one I can go back to over and over. How many times have you eaten out in the last week? The last two weeks? The last month? More than you probably would like to admit — which is most of America. Take a look at your credit card statement and see where your money is being spent. How much of your bill involves eating out? While eating out can be a fun way to celebrate and enjoy someone else's cooking occasionally, doing it on a frequent basis can cost a lot — not just in dollars but also in health. Cooking at home as much as possible is going to save you the most time and the most money. Plus, cooking at home allows you to control the ingredients.
- Meal planning eliminates decision fatigue and stress. I cannot stress this one enough. We have so many decisions to make in a day that start from the moment we wake up, and what to make for dinner is one of them. It's not often a simple decision either, because you have to take into account the schedules of everyone living in the household, the budget, the time, the ingredients you have on hand, and more. It really isn't a simple decision. But let me help you by giving you a simplified approach to meal planning that will have you always knowing what's for dinner.
- Cooking becomes fun! This is definitely true when you have a plan and when you look at cooking as a way to feed the soul of your family. Imagine what it's like to sit around the table with your family, and everyone is enjoying the food and having a good time. These are the memories you will want to cherish forever. I speak from experience now that one of my children has left the nest. You will wish for more time with them, and dinner is the perfect opportunity to create more time together.

What's next?

In the next chapter, I'm going to lay out your menu plan for you, with a weekly option as well as a monthly option. I'm going to share with you an essential kitchen tool list that makes cooking fast and easy and an essential pantry stocking list of things you'll need to make these meals come together. And bonus — I've prepared a shopping list for the menu plan, that you can even program and save into your favorite online grocery delivery location, so they can shop the ingredients for you.

Are you ready to get started with strategies that make every dinner a winner? Are you ready to have less stress in the kitchen and take some of the pressure off of a long day? Are you ready to finally have a plan and stop overcomplicating dinner while putting something healthy on the table? Then turn the page, and let's get started.

CHAPTER TWO

Mom's Forever Dinner Plan

Food tastes better when you eat it

with your family."

~Unknown

Now you know the power of meal planning, and how it can truly change your life and even your mindset about cooking. You have learned about the myths of meal planning, the mindset that can help you become a kitchen rockstar, and the lessons that you can take with you as you cook your way to more joy in the kitchen. This is not about adding one more thing you have to do in a day, but shifting your perspective on how it gets done that leads to more joy in your life.

When I first started delving into meal planning for my family, I took out a big stack of thick cookbooks and a pad of post-it notes and started putting a note on every recipe I wanted to try. I sat down on the couch for two hours, stared at pictures of the recipes, read through the ingredients, and felt overwhelmed. After using up the entire pad of post-it notes, I knew this plan wasn't going to work. It was taking way too long to come up with new recipe ideas, and it was going to take even longer to make these recipes all come together in some neat calendar system I had in my mind. And because trying those recipes required plotting them into some type of system that didn't exist, well, that meant I had more work to do.

The next step I took was taking a sheet of paper and making a list of all the recipes I made that my family enjoyed. They had to be easy to prepare on any given weeknight, they had to taste good, and they had to be mostly healthy too. Once I prepared that list, I drew out a graph on paper that resembled a calendar. This became the first cycle menu I tried to implement, but I ran into some issues because all the preparation was taking way longer than it should have.

Finally, I realized that the key to meal planning with success was using the right tools to make the meals I really wanted to prepare — meals that were tasty, fast, easy, and healthy. Exploring new kitchen tools and recipes as a Pampered Chef consultant blew me away. In my initial kit, I received a pizza stone and it made me remember those weekly pizza nights we would have growing up, where my mom made homemade pizza on a pizza stone. The electric pressure cooker launched and it was super intimidating to me until I tried my first recipe. The air fryer was another one of those items that made me wonder whether I really needed another appliance in the kitchen. But as a registered dietitian, I knew it could make things my family enjoyed healthier, and I knew the air fryer would definitely be faster.

Because of these kitchen tools, I discovered how the right tools really make the meal. Meaning, the right tools could be the assistant in the kitchen that I didn't have before. It quite honestly changed how I cook and revolutionized the process of meal planning and meal preparation for me. That's why I am so excited to share this meal planning technique with you.

First, a little quiz to help you gain a sense of direction of where you are now and where you want to be. Take this quick assessment and record your honest answers on the next page:

Kitchen Quiz:

1. What is the tool you use most often in your kitchen to make dinner?
2. How often do you serve breaded foods for dinner? How often do you head to the grocery store to get a rotisserie chicken?
3. Thinking about the last 7 nights, how often have you eaten out for dinner? If so, what was it?
4. What are your all-time favorite comfort foods? What types of meals are you naturally drawn to tearing out of a magazine or pinning on Pinterest?
5. Do you have a weekly family night where everyone hangs out together intentionally?

Answers:

1. If your most favorite tool is slow, then we need to speed things up for you. Chapter 3 will be a game changer for you.
2. If you love fried foods, then Chapter 4 is going to be your favorite, because I share how to make them healthier.
3. If you have favorites from restaurants, you will definitely love Chapter 5 where I help you recreate restaurant favorites at home.
4. If comfort foods like casseroles and hotdishes are your favorites, then Chapter 6 will give you some new ideas.
5. If you have a weekly family night, or even if you don't, I am going to make that even more impactful with a simple meal that you can make every week in Chapter 7.

To dig even deeper, answer these questions:

- What are your family's top favorite types of foods?
- If you could go into your pantry right now, what foods would be in there?
- What are your health goals?

These three questions are more of a value alignment. If your family's favorite foods aren't meeting your health goals, it is time to take a look at things to see what changes can be made. My hope is that by changing how you "do dinner" each night, that your family's favorite foods and your health goals will more closely align.

Quick Kitchen Audit

To set yourself up for success with the menu planning strategy I am sharing with you, go to your kitchen pantry right now and put a check mark by each of the items you have below:

Pantry Essentials:

Pantry Fruits & Vegetables

- Applesauce
- Mandarin Oranges
- Pineapple Tidbits
- Low Sodium Canned Vegetables (corn, green beans, carrots)
- Reduced Sodium Tomato Products (Sauce, Paste, Diced Tomatoes, Fire-Roasted Tomatoes, Crushed Tomatoes)
- Marinara Sauce
- Pizza Sauce
- Salsa
- Dried Cranberries/Raisins

Beans & Grains

- Black Beans (low sodium canned)
- Cannellini Beans (low sodium canned)
- Kidney Beans (low sodium canned)
- Refried Beans (low sodium/fat)
- Pasta (all shapes - whole grain if possible)
- Rice: Jasmine/Brown Rice/Wild/Long-Grain
- Whole Grain Bread
- Whole Grain Tortillas
- Oatmeal
- Breadcrumbs (Italian/Panko/Plain - Whole Grain)

Oils & Vinegars

- White Vinegar
- Red Wine Vinegar
- Apple Cider Vinegar
- Sherry Vinegar
- Extra Virgin Olive Oil
- Avocado Oil
- Canola Oil

Spices and Herbs

- Black Pepper
- Garlic Powder
- Ground Ginger
- Cinnamon
- CayennePaprika (sweet & smoked)
- Oregano
- Chili Powder
- Ground Thyme
- Dried Rosemary
- Ground Cumin
- Ground Nutmeg
- Ground Cloves
- Italian Seasoning
- Bay Leaves
- Spice Blends (noted on page 21)
- Reduced Sodium Fajita and Taco Seasoning

Pantry essentials, continued:

Flavor Boosters

- Salad Dressings (lower sodium)
- Vanilla Extract
- Olives
- Maple Syrup
- Honey
- Unbleached All-Purpose Flour
- Bread Flour
- Baking Powder
- Baking Soda
- Cornstarch
- Evaporated Fat Free Milk
- Reduced Sodium Cream of Chicken/Mushroom and Chicken Gumbo Soups

- Canned Chilis
- Reduced Sodium Broth
- Sweet Thai Chili Sauce
- Reduced Sodium Soy Sauce
- Pesto Sauce
- Toasted Sesame Oil
- Worcestershire Sauce
- Sriracha Sauce
- Barbecue Sauce
- Dijon Mustard
- Ketchup
- Mustard
- Jam
- Mayonnaise
- Pickles

Countertop/Dry Storage Fruits & Vegetables

- bananas [store away from other fruit to prevent over-ripening]
- melons [until ripe]
- pineapple [until ripe]
- tomatoes
- pears [until ripe]
- winter squash [spaghetti, butternut]
- potatoes
- sweet potatoes
- garlic
- onions

Nuts & Seeds

- Peanut Butter
- Walnuts
- Pecans
- Chia Seeds
- Pumpkin Seeds

Refrigerator Essentials

Refrigerated Vegetables

- romaine
- spinach
- mushrooms
- carrots
- bell peppers
- broccoli
- cucumbers
- cauliflower
- zucchini
- cucumbers
- shredded cabbage (coleslaw mix)
- celery
- winter squash
- fresh cilantro
- fresh basil

Fruits

- apples
- oranges
- clementines
- grapefruit
- strawberries
- blueberries
- raspberries
- grapes
- kiwis
- lemons
- limes
- ripe avocado
- cherries
- peaches
- pineapple
- blackberries
- pears
- 100% juice puree

Proteins

- fish (cod/salmon)
- chicken (breasts/thighs/tenders)
- chicken wings
- 3-4 pound whole chicken
- eggs
- pork tenderloin/roast
- lean ground beef
- turkey breast/ground turkey
- sirloin steak (for beef stew
- turkey sausage crumbles (pre-cooked)
- deli meats (ham, turkey, roast beef)

Dairy

- Greek yogurt (plain/flavored)
- milks [dairy/non-dairy]
- cottage cheese
- cheese block/slices (Swiss, cheddar, mozzarella, Parmesan, Colby, Muenster)
- half & half
- butter

Freezer

- frozen fish fillets (cod and salmon)
- peeled, deveined shrimp
- proteins (ground beef, chicken, turkey, pork as noted in protein section)
- whole grain bread
- whole grain waffles
- vegetables including spinach, corn, green beans, cauliflower, broccoli, peas and carrots
- fruits - pineapple, strawberries, mango, berries
- frozen tator tots
- light whipped topping (for yogurt dip)

Additional Seasonings to Make Cooking Even Easier*:

- All-Purpose Dill Mix
- Asian Seasoning Mix
- Bell Pepper Herb Rub
- Chipotle Rub
- Crushed Peppercorn and Garlic Rub
- Everything Bagel Seasoning
- Garlic and Herb Rub
- Greek Rub
- Italian Seasoning Mix
- Jamaican Jerk Rub
- Lemon Garlic Rub
- Rosemary Herb Seasoning Mix
- Rotisserie Seasoning
- Smoky Applewood Rub
- Southwestern Seasoning Mix
- Sweet Basil Rub
- Tex-Mex Rub

When you are set up well with the right ingredients, you will cook much more frequently and enjoy the process, as everything will be right at your fingertips.

Top Kitchen Tools to Make Meals Easier:

The right tools can make you a better, more confident cook in the kitchen. You will not only get things done faster and more efficiently, but you will have the desire to cook more often for your family. Here is a list of all the tools I recommend.

To Speed Up Meal Prep:
- Electric food processor (bonus if it is cordless)
- Hand mixer (bonus if it is cordless)
- Immersion blender (bonus if it is cordless)
- Rapid prep mandolin (a safe version that won't cut your fingers)
- Food chopper
- Veggie spiralizer
- Manual food processor
- Adjustable graters (for cheese)
- Vegetable slicer
- Vegetable peeler

To Speed Up Cook Time and Allow You to Leave the Kitchen:
- Pressure Cooker
- Air Fryer
- Cooking Blender
- Electric Grill and Griddle

Basics Every Kitchen Needs:

- Non-Stick Cookware (Look for POFA-free cookware. POFA is a chemical associated with teflon coatings.)
- Cast Iron Skillet
- Stainless Steel Non-Stick Skillet with Lid
- Grill Pan
- Dutch Oven (Microwave Safe is a plus)
- Roasting Pan
- Non-Stick Half Sheet Pan/Modular Sheet Pans
- Pizza Stone
- High Quality Knives like a Chef's Knife, Utility Knife or Santoku Knife, and Paring Knife
- Cutting Boards — made from high density polypropylene (not glass or wood)
- Cutting Mats
- Silicone Scrapers
- Whisk Set
- Spatula
- Tongs
- Wooden Spoons (Bamboo is a plus for easy clean up in the dishwasher)
- Mixing Bowl Set
- Microwave-Safe Cookware
- Leak-Proof Storage Containers
- Prep Bowls
- Measuring Cups and Spoons

Essential Meal Planning Strategy: The Forever Dinner Plan

Now, let's map out my strategy that will change how you look at meal planning. The first step is creating your menu map. Just answer the questions quickly below thinking of life right now (not two months down the road):

Your Menu Planning Map:

1. Which night is your busiest evening? → This is your pressure cooker day.
2. Which night are you out of energy most often? → This is air fryer night.
3. Which night do you normally go out to eat because of schedules or people's requests? → This is grill/griddle night.
4. Which night is the night you just want to put your feet up after a long day? → A one pot meal is where it's at.
5. Which night is the night you want to designate as family night? → This is pizza night.

See how easy this strategy is? I hope that was easy for you. Of course, what you answered today may be different in the future, and when that time comes, just ask yourself these questions again to realign things for yourself. I know what it's like to come home after being in meetings all day and not having the energy to make a decision about dinner. This simple strategy streamlines the process for you — now dinner matches your lifestyle, rather than your life running you through the drive-through.

Once you have your menu planning map figured out, it's time to plot it into your chart. For example, if Mondays are your busiest night because of parent–teacher association meetings or a church meeting, that should be a pressure cooking night because you can put all the ingredients in the pot and set it and forget it, and not too long later, you will have a meal for the family. If Thursdays tend to be the night you grab a burger and fries at the local restaurant, then make that your grill/griddle night. You can make that hamburger healthier at home and turn it into a fun burger bar where everyone gets to top it with what they like, and you can even make your own smoothies instead of milkshakes. Use your life as a guide to making the best map possible!

Here's an example for one week:

Busiest Night	Longest Day	Normally Out to Eat	Out of Energy	Family Night
Pressure Cooker Meal: Chapter Three	One Pot Meal: Chapter Six	Grill/Griddle Meal: Chapter Five	Air Fryer Meal: Chapter Four	Pizza Meal: Chapter Seven

Now let me apply this menu magic to six weeks of dinners so you can see how easy it is. Based on the rhythm I shared above, here's your six week plan:

Monday	Tuesday	Wednesday	Thursday	Friday
Hearty Minnesota Chili	Zesty Pasta Skillet	Panini Night	Crispy Chicken Tenders	Taco Pizza
Creamy Chicken Pesto Pasta	Taco Bubble Casserole	Slider Bar	Hawaiian Coconut Shrimp	BBQ Chicken Pizza
Egg Roll in a Bowl	Creamy Turkey and Noodles	Chicken Fajitas	Rotisserie Pork Tenderloin	Detroit Style Pizza
Burrito Bowl	Barbecues	Ginger Brown Sugar Glazed Salmon	Pizza Stromboli	Healthy Hawaiian Pizza
Spaghetti	Sheet Pan Dinner	Quesadillas	Crunchy Cod	Chicken Fajita Pizza
Beef Stew	General Tso Chicken Stir Fry	French Toast	Steak Kebabs	Italian Sausage Pesto Pizza

I also have side dishes mapped out for you based on the meal — just serve the side dish that corresponds with the main meal above (you will see these in each chapter) - the same side dish for that specific night of the week. Decision fatigue gone.

Salad	Fresh Vegetables and & Dip	Smoothie	Roasted Vegetables	Fresh Fruit and Dip

Now it's your turn — plot your week out. Name the day of the week that matches the following:

What is your busiest night:	What is your busiest night:	What is your busiest night:	What is your busiest night:	What is your busiest night:

Keep in mind, this menu planning map is to help you get through the weeknights. What you do on the weekend may be different. Many times there are places to go on the weekend, potlucks and picnics, or perhaps a meal that you cook for more than just your family. Use the weekend as a time to experiment with new recipes if you wish, or make old favorites. This system is to help you get through the week with recipes that are tasty, easy to make, take little time, and are healthy too.

Once you have your menu map made, it's time to fill it in with recipes. My hope is that my tried and true favorite recipes you find in this book will become favorites for your family too. And if that is the case, meal planning will be even easier for you. Of course, if you want to add in your own favorites, by all means, go ahead.

Recipe List:

Here are all the recipes in this book. Which of these recipes immediately jump out at you? Take a moment to circle or jot down which ones immediately appeal to you just by looking at their title.

Air Fryer Night:

- Crispy Chicken Tenders
- Crunchy Cod
- Hawaiian Coconut Shrimp
- Steak Kebabs
- Rotisserie Pork Tenderloin
- Rotisserie Chicken
- Pizza Stromboli
- Simple Side Dish: Mashed Potatoes and Roasted Vegetables

One Pot Meal Night:

- Barbecues
- General Tso Chicken Stir Fry
- Chicken Pot Pie
- Tater Tot Casserole
- Zesty Pasta Skillet
- California Chicken and Rice
- Taco Bubble Casserole
- Creamy Turkey and Noodles
- Sheet Pan Dinners
- Simple Side Dish: Fresh Vegetable Platter with Dip

Family Pizza Night:

- Homemade Pizza Dough Two Ways
- Barbecue Chicken Pizza
- Healthy Hawaiian Pizza
- Garden Fresh Pizza
- Italian Sausage Pesto Pizza
- Taco Pizza
- Chicken Fajita Pizza
- Detroit Style Pizza
- Thai Chicken Pizza
- Simple Side Dish: Fresh Fruit and Dip

Pressure Cooker Meals:

- Chicken Wild Rice Soup
- Broccoli Cheese Soup
- Hearty Minnesota Chili
- Spaghetti
- Fettuccini Alfredo with Chicken
- Creamy Chicken Pesto Pasta
- Egg Roll in a Bowl
- Burrito Bowls (Beef/Chicken)
- Beef Stew
- Macaroni and Cheese
- Simple Side Dish: Salad Mix and Match

Grill/Griddle Night:

- Panini Bar
- Smashed Slider Bar
- Quesadilla Bar
- Ginger Brown Sugar Glazed Salmon
- Chicken Fajitas
- French Toast for Dinner
- Side Dish: Smoothie

Now that you have circled what you are most interested in above, add your own favorites in the following categories. This way you can capture anything you already make and your family loves and incorporate those meals as well.

Are there any other pressure cooker dinners your family already loves?

1.

2.

3.

Are there any other recipes or foods you make in the air fryer that are healthier and your family enjoys?

1.

2.

3.

Are there any other restaurant meals you think need to be replicated?

1.

2.

3.

Any other top favorite one pot meals that are a must-have?

1.

2.

3.

Are there any other favorite types of pizza your family enjoys?

1.

2.

3.

Now, personalize your forever dinner plan!

1. From the pressure cooker recipes you circled, write down the six recipes you want to make into the column that matches the day of the week you find the busiest.
2. From the air fryer recipes you circled, write down the six recipes you want to make into the column that matches the day of the week when you feel the most out of energy.
3. From the grill/griddle night recipes you circled, write down the six recipes you want to make into the column that matches the day of the week you tend to find yourself rolling through the drive-through or eating out.
4. From the one pot meal night recipes you circled, write down the six recipes you want to make into the column that matches the day of the week you tend to find yourself having a long day.
5. From the pizza night recipes you circled, write down the six recipes you want to make into the column that matches the day of the week you are having a family night.

Once you have the chart below filled in, you will have a forever dinner plan. Sure — you can always add new recipes to the rotation, but you can feel confident in knowing that you have it all planned out and you will never have to think about it again.

My Forever Dinner Plan

Monday	Tuesday	Wednesday	Thursday	Friday

It's Done

Now that you have this simple plan to get dinner done, take a deep breath! How does it feel to have a strategy for dinner forever? How does it feel that you will be able to take back your time and remove decision fatigue in the busiest season of your life?

The following chapters are broken down by kitchen tool, and include the recipes you need for your menu map. At the end of the book, you can find extra recipe pages that are blank for you to include some of your own favorites so everything is all in one place.

I hope you feel that I have done the heavy lifting for you, that you are now free to "roam about the cabin," meaning tend to the things that matter while the tools are cooking the meals for you. I am so excited to be helping you bring more joy to your kitchen and to your life in this way!

Before you move on to the next page, keep this in mind. You will have a choice to make — you can implement everything right away and jumpstart yourself instantly with this plan. That will give you the best results. But I understand that for some, that can be overwhelming, so you may choose to take the plan in baby steps, where you focus on one chapter a week until you make it through. Either way — finish it. This is the plan that can help you with all the goals you have for your family's dinners. You will feel like a load has been lifted off your shoulders because you will finally feel in control of the kitchen.

Resources on my website:

Download the Dinner, Done! Planner with printable copies of the six-week, done-for-you menu map, a blank menu map, grocery list, recommended tools and seasonings too.

CHAPTER THREE

Pressure Cooker Recipes

All great change in America begins
at the dinner table.

~Ronald Reagan

I am so excited for you to begin with this first step.Remember, it all starts with this one question: Which night of the week is your busiest night? Look at your weeks ahead for the next month. Do you have a recurring meeting or event that always happens that same night of the week? Do you have a night of the week that feels chaotic with evening responsibilities at home? Whatever night tends to feel the most time-constrained at dinner is the night to start with for this chapter. Keep it simple and stay flexible. Because this is the busy weeknight chapter, you are going to hear all about pressure cooking. Pressure cooking is something that has revolutionized my cooking life. Growing up, my mom had a stovetop-style pressure cooker, and it was the style that had the hissing disk on the top of the lid that could blow off at any time. We were warned of this as children, so we didn't really stand in the kitchen when this type of cooking was going on. Fast forward a couple of decades to when I was feeling frazzled on weeknights trying to make a healthy meal for my family. I thought my only option was a slow cooker. But, as the name suggests, it was slow and required thawing meat a day or two ahead of time and getting up early in the morning to prep the meal. On top of getting myself and my kids ready in the morning, it just wasn't practical. When electric pressure cookers became popular, I was still resistant to this type of cooking method given my "unsafe" experience as a kid. However, a year after I became a kitchen consultant, my company released an electric pressure cooker. I knew I was going to have to at least try it even though I was hesitant. Little did I know that this purchase would change everything in the kitchen for me.

When it showed up on my doorstep, I was intimidated and afraid that it would blow up in my kitchen when I used it. I thought I might as well see what the fuss was about as I had heard that even if your meat is frozen, it would still cook it 70% faster and have the same tenderness and flavor as if it had cooked all day. So, I marched down our steps to the deep freeze and pulled out a frozen pork tenderloin, unwrapped it, and put it inside the pressure cooker with one cup of water. I set it for the beef/pork setting and about 45 minutes later (while I helped my kids with their homework, made a fresh salad, and enjoyed a quick walk around the block), it was finished cooking!

When I opened the lid, not only was I blown away by the smell, but I stuck my fork into the tenderloin and noticed how tender it truly was. I quickly shredded it up for pulled pork sandwiches and had my aha moment. I didn't have to think that far in advance and I could still put a healthy meal on the table in minutes. That was the day I fell in love with the pressure cooker.

Since then, I have cooked a hundred if not a thousand times in my pressure cooker. It has saved me so many times in making a meal when I had no plan at all, when I forgot to thaw the meat, or when I just needed to speed up the process of mealtime altogether because of our schedule. The meal options are endless and I am including my family's top favorites here so you can streamline dinner, stop feeling bad about not having a plan, and still come out looking like a kitchen rockstar. I love that it cooks foods 70% faster, all while not having to babysit the pot as you would ordinarily if you cooked any of these recipes on the stovetop or in the oven. Plus the pot is dishwasher safe, so it's easy to clean up as well.

6 Pressure Cooking Tips:

1. Make sure you keep the same order of the ingredients when you are adding them to the pot, as the order often serves a purpose.
2. Make sure you measure any liquids that are important to the recipe. This is not the time to eyeball it, as you want to be sure you have enough liquid inside the pot for it to work correctly.
3. Make sure the steam valve is closed when you begin the cooking process, and make sure your silicone ring is in good working order — meaning it's not overly stretched out. Deep clean your pressure cooker at least once a month. You can find a video tutorial of this on my website. It's fast and easy, and doing the maintenance is really worth it to keep your pressure cooker working long term.
4. When you are making pasta, weigh the pasta in ounces. Once you know the ounces, just double that number, and that's how many ounces of water you will add to the pot to get the pasta to cook up appropriately without having to drain anything off.
5. Pay attention to the max load level inside the pot. Your ingredients should never be higher than that line; things will expand as they are cooking, including liquid.
6. Pay attention to whether the recipe tells you to use natural release or quick release of the steam at the end of cooking. Natural release is often used with meats to let them rest for a few minutes and finish the tenderizing process, and sometimes with soups to let the liquid settle down in the pot so it doesn't spurt out. For natural release, you simply let the pot sit after it is done cooking for the time the recipe states. Once that time elapses, you simply press the button to release any remaining steam. Quick release is where you press the button immediately after the cooking process is finished. It will take 30-60 seconds or sometimes more to release all the pressure built up inside. Do not lift the lid off until the indicator drops to tell you that all pressure has been released.

Some helpful tools in this chapter include:

- Electric Pressure Cooker
- Manual Food Processor (for dicing onions, peppers, and celery)
- Salad Chopper (for cutting cooked chicken in the pot)
- Mix & Chop (for crumbling ground beef in the pot)

Chicken & Wild Rice Soup

PREP TIME: 5 MIN   PRESSURE COOKING TIME: 30 MIN   ADDITIONAL TIME: 5 MIN

SERVINGS: 6

This recipe is one of our favorite soup recipes to prepare whether it's cold outside or not. It has a lot of vegetables and you don't need to cook the chicken in advance. Plus, you don't need to cut up the chicken in advance, especially if you have one of my favorite tools, the Salad Chopper.

Ingredients

2 tablespoons olive oil or butter

1 onion, diced

1 cup diced celery (2-3 large stalks)

1 cup sliced carrots (2 large carrots)

28 ounces chicken broth (low sodium preferred)

2 large chicken breasts, uncooked

6 ounce package long grain & wild rice mixture (with half of the seasoning packet, like Uncle Ben's or something similar)

½ teaspoon salt

½ teaspoon black pepper

2 ounces lite cream cheese

1 cup milk

1 cup half and half

Directions

1. Select the "Sear" function on your pressure cooker and let it heat up for 2 minutes. Add the olive oil or butter to the pot, followed by the onions, celery, and carrots. Stir, and cook for 3-4 minutes.

2. Add the broth, chicken, rice mix, salt, and pepper to the pot.

3. Lock the lid in place and press "Custom", adjust the time to 9 minutes, and press "start." When the cook time ends, wait 5 minutes, then press the "Steam Release" button until the pressure indicator valve drops down and the lid is safe to open.

4. Use salad choppers to quickly chop through chicken right in the pot (alternatively, remove the chicken and cut it up on a cutting board).

5. Add the cream cheese and stir until melted. Add the milk and half and half and leave it on the "warming" setting until the soup is heated through (but do not boil). Season your soup with additional salt and pepper to taste. Enjoy with crusty bread and a salad.

Nutrition Facts	Amount/serving	% Daily Value*	Amount/serving	% Daily Value*	
	Total Fat 11.4g	17%	Total Carbohydrates 35g	11%	* The percent Daily Value (DV) tells you how much a nutrient in a serving of food contributes to a daily diet. 2,000 calories a day is used for general nutrition advice.
6 servings	Saturated Fat 4.2g	20%	Dietary Fiber 2g	9%	
	Trans Fat 0.0g		Total Sugars 6g		
Calories per serving 343	Cholesterol 61mg	20%			
	Sodium 489mg	21%	Protein 23g		
	Vitamin D 1mcg 8% · Calcium 165mg 16% · Iron 4mg 20% · Potassium 515mg 10%				

Broccoli Cheese Soup

PREP TIME: 10 MIN   PRESSURE COOKING TIME: 2 MIN   ADDITIONAL TIME: 20 MIN

SERVINGS: 6

If you love cheesy soup with vegetables, then you will love this recipe. It's easy to make and very tasty. And can you imagine a 2-minute pressure cooking time? That's why pressure cooking is so great for busy nights.

Ingredients

5 tablespoons olive oil or butter, divided

1 small onion, diced

3 cloves garlic, pressed

¼ cup all purpose flour

1 cup milk

1 cup half and half

20 ounces chicken broth (low sodium preferred)

3 cups broccoli florets, chopped small

1 large carrot, sliced thinly

1 teaspoon salt

½ teaspoon black pepper

½ teaspoon paprika

8 oz extra sharp cheddar cheese, shredded

Directions

1. Select the "Sear" function on your pressure cooker and let the pot heat for 2 minutes. Add 1 tablespoon of olive oil or butter and the onion and garlic to the pot. Stir and cook for 2 minutes.
2. Add the remaining 4 tablespoons of olive oil or butter to the pot so it melts. Add flour and stir well to combine the flour with the butter. Cook for 1-2 minutes or until the flour starts to bubble. Gradually whisk in broth.
3. Add broccoli, carrots, salt, pepper, and paprika to the pot. Select "Custom," set the cook time for 2 minutes, and press start.
4. When pressure cooking has finished, press the steam release button immediately, and wait until the pressure indicator valve drops down and the lid is safe to open. Remove the lid. Pour in milk and half and half, whisking constantly. Stir in the shredded cheese. Serve with crusty bread and a salad.

Nutrition Facts		Amount/serving	% Daily Value*	Amount/serving	% Daily Value*	
		Total Fat 28.3g	43%	Total Carbohydrates 18g	6%	* The percent Daily Value (DV) tells you how much a nutrient in a serving of food contributes to a daily diet. 2,000 calories a day is used for general nutrition advice.
		Saturated Fat 11.2g	56%	Dietary Fiber 3g	11%	
6 servings		Trans Fat 0.0g		Total Sugars 6g		
		Cholesterol 55mg	18%			
Calories	388	Sodium 718mg	31%	Protein 17g		
per serving						
		Vitamin D 0mcg 0% · Calcium 351mg 35% · Iron 1mg 5% · Potassium 418mg 8%				

Hearty Minnesota Chili

PREP TIME: 5 MIN   PRESSURE COOKING TIME: 8 MIN   ADDITIONAL TIME: 20 MIN

SERVINGS: 6

When my kids are home, they request this recipe no matter if it is summer or winter. It's a recipe that has evolved from a chili that I grew up eating, and it easily becomes a hearty meal with a touch of sweetness from the ketchup and oregano. The quickest way to crumble the beef is with a Mix & Chop.

Ingredients

1 pound lean ground beef

1 large onion, diced

2 bell peppers, diced

1 teaspoon oregano

2 teaspoons chili powder

½ cup ketchup

1 (14.5 oz) can petite diced tomatoes

12 ounces beef broth (low sodium preferred)

1 (14.5 oz) can kidney beans or black beans (reduced sodium or no added salt preferred), rinsed and drained

Directions

1. Select the "Sear" setting on your pressure cooker and heat the pot for 2 minutes. Add ground beef, onion, and bell peppers. Stir and crumble ground beef for 2-3 minutes. The meat will not be cooked all the way through — we are just looking for it to start to brown.

2. Add oregano, chili powder, ketchup, tomatoes, beef broth, and beans. Select "Custom" setting and adjust the time to 8 minutes. Lock the lid and press "Start".

3. When the cooking time is finished, let the pressure cooker sit for 5 minutes, and then press the steam release button to release the pressure until the pressure indicator valve drops down and the lid is safe to open. Remove the lid and enjoy with grilled cheese or cornbread and a salad.

Nutrition Facts	Amount/serving	% Daily Value*	Amount/serving	% Daily Value*	
6 servings	**Total Fat** 8.8g	13%	**Total Carbohydrates** 23g	7%	* The percent Daily Value (DV) tells you how much a nutrient in a serving of food contributes to a daily diet. 2,000 calories a day is used for general nutrition advice.
	Saturated Fat 4.5g	22%	Dietary Fiber 8g	32%	
	Trans Fat 0.4g		Total Sugars 7g		
Calories 311 per serving	**Cholesterol** 66mg	22%			
	Sodium 280mg	12%	**Protein** 26g		

Vitamin D 0mcg 0% · Calcium 93mg 9% · Iron 403mg 2241% · Potassium 850mg 18%

Spaghetti

PREP TIME: 2 MIN   PRESSURE COOKING TIME: 5 MIN   ADDITIONAL TIME: 15 MIN

SERVINGS: 6

An all-time favorite made even better because of the 5-minute cooking time. Seriously, I haven't cooked a pot of spaghetti on the stovetop in years thanks to this recipe. Plus, leftovers are minimal every time.

Ingredients

- 1 pound ground beef
- 1 tablespoon Italian Seasoning
- 1 medium onion, diced
- 8 oz spaghetti dry pasta
- 1 (26 ounce) jar marinara pasta sauce
- 16 ounces water

Directions

1. Select the "Sear" setting on your pressure cooker and heat for 2 minutes. Add ground beef, Italian seasoning, and onion and cook for 2 minutes, crumbling meat as you stir.
2. Break pasta in half and lay a criss cross pattern inside the pot on top of the meat mixture. Add the marinara sauce and top with water. Select "custom" setting and adjust time to 5 minutes with the lid locked in place. Press "Start".
3. When cooking time is finished, press the steam release button until the pressure indicator drops and the lid is safe to open. Mixture will be slightly watery, but stir and it will evaporate quickly due to the high temperatures. Enjoy with crusty bread and a salad.

Nutrition Facts	Amount/serving	% Daily Value*	Amount/serving	% Daily Value*	
6 servings	**Total Fat** 19.2g	29%	**Total Carbohydrates** 37g	12%	* The percent Daily Value (DV) tells you how much a nutrient in a serving of food contributes to a daily diet. 2,000 calories a day is used for general nutrition advice.
	Saturated Fat 5.5g	27%	Dietary Fiber 3g	10%	
	Trans Fat 0.4g		Total Sugars 6g		
Calories **441** per serving	**Cholesterol** 66mg	22%			
	Sodium 471mg	20%	**Protein** 27g		
	Vitamin D 0mcg 0% · Calcium 48mg 4% · Iron 3mg 19% · Potassium 742mg 15%				

Fettuccine Alfredo with Chicken

PREP TIME: 5 MIN   PRESSURE COOKING TIME: 8 MIN   ADDITIONAL TIME: 15 MIN

SERVINGS: 6

This will be the easiest alfredo you will ever make. Be sure to follow the order precisely so everything cooks up as it should. If you have pasta lovers in your house, this will be a favorite!

Ingredients

12 ounces chicken broth (low sodium preferred)

12 ounces evaporated skim milk or half and half

1 garlic clove, pressed

8 ounces fettuccine pasta

1 pound chicken breasts, uncooked

1 cup Parmesan cheese, freshly grated

Black pepper, to taste

Directions

1. Add the chicken broth, cream, and garlic to the pot. Do not stir.
2. Next, add the pasta broken in half, laying it in a criss cross fashion. Try to submerge the pasta in the broth and cream mixture.
3. Top with chicken breasts (frozen chicken breasts are okay too); chicken does not need to be submerged.
4. Select the "Custom" setting on your pressure cooker, and adjust time to 8 minutes with the lid locked in place. Press "Start".
5. Once cooking is finished, let the pot sit for 8 additional minutes — this is called natural release of steam. If at the end of 8 minutes the pressure indicator is still elevated, press the steam release button to release any additional steam until the pressure indicator drops.
6. Open lid and use Salad Chopper to chop chicken quickly in the pot (alternatively, remove chicken and dice on a cutting board), add cheese, and stir. Allow to sit 1-2 additional minutes to allow sauce to thicken with the cheese. Enjoy with crusty bread and a salad.

Nutrition Facts	Amount/serving	% Daily Value*	Amount/serving	% Daily Value*	
6 servings	**Total Fat** 6.9g	10%	**Total Carbohydrates** 36g	11%	* The percent Daily Value (DV) tells you how much a nutrient in a serving of food contributes to a daily diet. 2,000 calories a day is used for general nutrition advice.
	Saturated Fat 3.3g	16%	Dietary Fiber 1g	4%	
	Trans Fat 0.0g		Total Sugars 7g		
	Cholesterol 53mg	17%			
Calories 342 per serving	**Sodium** 374mg	16%	**Protein** 30g		
	Vitamin D 2mcg 20% · Calcium 364mg 36% · Iron 4mg 22% · Potassium 360mg 7%				

Creamy Chicken Pesto Pasta

PREP TIME: 10 MIN   PRESSURE COOKING TIME: 5 MIN   ADDITIONAL TIME: 25 MIN

SERVINGS: 6

One of my favorite sauces is pesto sauce, because I love making it with fresh basil from my garden. In the winter, I use jarred pesto sauce, and it's delicious too. Your kitchen will quickly become your family's favorite Italian restaurant.

Ingredients

3½ cups water

1 pound dry penne pasta

1 pound chicken breasts

1 tablespoon olive oil or butter

½ teaspoon salt

3 cups spinach leaves

1 cup halved cherry tomatoes

½ cup basil pesto sauce

¼ cup cream cheese

2 garlic cloves, pressed

1 teaspoon black pepper

Additional topping: shredded Parmesan cheese, as desired

Directions

1. Pour water into the pot and add pasta, chicken, olive oil or butter, and salt. Ensure pasta is submerged in water. Select the "custom" setting, adjust time to 5 minutes, lock the lid in place, and press "Start".

2. When cooking time is finished, press the steam release button and let the pressure release until the pressure indicator drops. Open the lid and remove 1 ladle of water from the pot (approximately ¼ cup). Quickly dice chicken in the pot with the Salad Chopper.

3. Select the "Sear" function and add spinach, tomatoes, pesto, cream cheese, garlic, and black pepper to the pot along with the pasta and chicken. Stir frequently and cook for an additional 2 minutes.

4. Divide pasta mixture into bowls and top with Parmesan cheese. Serve with salad.

Nutrition Facts	Amount/serving	% Daily Value*	Amount/serving	% Daily Value*	
6 servings	Total Fat 21.3g	32%	Total Carbohydrates 61g	20%	* The percent Daily Value (DV) tells you how much a nutrient in a serving of food contributes to a daily diet. 2,000 calories a day is used for general nutrition advice.
	Saturated Fat 3.1g	15%	Dietary Fiber 3g	12%	
	Trans Fat 0.0g		Total Sugars 4g		
Calories 547 per serving	Cholesterol 45mg	15%			
	Sodium 439mg	19%	Protein 27g		
	Vitamin D 0mcg 3% · Calcium 83mg 8% · Iron 7mg 36% · Potassium 458mg 9%				

Egg Roll in a Bowl

PREP TIME: 5 MIN   PRESSURE COOKING TIME: 0 MIN   ADDITIONAL TIME: 10 MIN
(YES, YOU READ THAT RIGHT)

SERVINGS: 6

This recipe incorporates lots of vegetables, and yes, it will be loved by your family! The flavor of the sauce is delicious and tastes exactly like an egg roll without the fried shell. We have been making this for years.

Ingredients

1 tablespoon olive or canola oil

½ yellow onion, diced

1 pound ground turkey sausage (hot variety)

2 red or green bell peppers, diced

1 package (14 ounces) coleslaw mix

Sauce:

¼ small yellow onion, minced

3 tablespoons reduced sodium soy sauce

1 tablespoon honey

1 teaspoon Sriracha sauce

Optional serving idea and toppings: Prepared jasmine rice, chow mein noodles, green onions, cilantro

Directions

1. Set your pressure cooker to the "Sear" setting and press start. Let the pot heat up for 2 minutes. Add oil, onions, sausage, and peppers and cook for 2-3 minutes, or until the meat is slightly brown (not all the way cooked). Press the "Cancel" button.

2. Add the bag of coleslaw mix — do not stir. Mix together sauce ingredients and pour sauce mixture over the top of the coleslaw. Place the lid on the pressure cooker, press the "Custom" setting and adjust time to "0 minutes." (Yes — I do mean zero). Press "Start".

3. Once finished pressure cooking, press the steam release button and let steam release until the red indicator drops and the lid is safe to open. Open the lid, stir, and serve over rice, topped with optional toppings. Serve with salad.

Nutrition Facts	Amount/serving	% Daily Value*	Amount/serving	% Daily Value*	
6 servings	**Total Fat** 8.5g	13%	**Total Carbohydrates** 56g	18%	* The percent Daily Value (DV) tells you how much a nutrient in a serving of food contributes to a daily diet. 2,000 calories a day is used for general nutrition advice.
	Saturated Fat 1.8g	9%	Dietary Fiber 4g	14%	
	Trans Fat 0.3g		Total Sugars 49g		
Calories 354 per serving	**Cholesterol** 57mg	18%			
	Sodium 785mg	34%	**Protein** 16g		
	Vitamin D 0mcg 0% · Calcium 48mg 4% · Iron 401mg 2228% · Potassium 481mg 10%				

Chicken Burrito Bowls

PREP TIME: 10 MIN   PRESSURE COOKING TIME: 15 MIN   ADDITIONAL TIME: 25 MIN

SERVINGS: 6

This is a healthy recipe that's fast and full of flavor. Plus it's customizable and everyone can choose which toppings they want to put on their bowl. You can even swap the chicken for ground beef if you'd like.

Ingredients

1 red bell pepper, sliced thinly into strips

1 yellow onion, sliced thinly

1 pound boneless, skinless chicken breasts

1 (14 ounce) can no-salt-added black beans

1 (14 ounce) can no-salt-added corn

2 tablespoons chipotle rub or fajita seasoning (or reduced sodium taco seasoning)

1 cup salsa

Additional Ingredients for the Bowl:

Cooked jasmine or brown rice

Romaine lettuce, thinly sliced

Cherry tomatoes, halved

1 ripe avocado, peeled, pitted, and sliced

Freshly grated cheddar cheese

Fresh cilantro, minced

Tortilla strips

Directions

1. Place pepper, onion, chicken, beans, corn, and seasoning into the bottom of your pressure cooker pot in order listed. Add salsa. Place the lid on the pressure cooker, and press the "Chicken/Poultry" button. Press "Start." (This pre-set button has a 15 minute pressure cooking time.)

2. Once finished pressure cooking, press the steam release button and let steam release until the indicator drops. Open the lid, use the salad chopper to chop chicken right in the pot (alternatively, remove chicken and dice on a clean cutting board). Stir ingredients together in the pot and serve over rice with additional toppings.

Homemade Cilantro Ranch Dressing:

1 lime, juiced

½ cup low-fat buttermilk

⅔ cup plain non-fat Greek yogurt

1 teaspoon Dijon mustard

1 tablespoon fresh cilantro, minced

⅛ teaspoon each of black pepper and salt

2 garlic cloves, pressed

Nutrition Facts	Amount/serving	% Daily Value*	Amount/serving	% Daily Value*	
6 servings	**Total Fat** 2.6g	3%	**Total Carbohydrates** 31g	10%	* The percent Daily Value (DV) tells you how much a nutrient in a serving of food contributes to a daily diet. 2,000 calories a day is used for general nutrition advice.
	Saturated Fat 0.7g	3%	Dietary Fiber 8g	30%	
	Trans Fat 0.0g		Total Sugars 8g		
Calories per serving **223**	**Cholesterol** 40mg	13%			
	Sodium 576mg	25%	**Protein** 22g		
	Vitamin D 0mcg 3% · Calcium 44mg 4% · Iron 205mg 1136% · Potassium 582mg 12%				

Beef Stew

PREP TIME: 11 MIN   PRESSURE COOKING TIME: 45 MIN   ADDITIONAL TIME: 46 MIN

SERVINGS: 6

This is midwest food at its best. I have never made a faster beef stew that was still so tender. This will please the heartiest of eaters and it's great served over mashed potatoes or biscuits.

Ingredients

2 tablespoons canola oil

1½ pounds boneless top sirloin (cut into 1-inch cubes)

¼ cup all-purpose flour

½ teaspoon salt

½ teaspoon black pepper

2 medium yellow onions, diced

1 teaspoon dried ground thyme

1 garlic clove, pressed

1½ cups low-sodium beef broth

1 teaspoon Worcestershire sauce

2 bay leaves

2 cups frozen mixed peas and carrots

To serve: biscuits or mashed potatoes

Directions

1. Combine flour, salt, and pepper and sprinkle over beef. Toss to coat. Press the "Sear" button on your pressure cooker and let the pot heat for 2 minutes. Add oil and then add the beef mixture. Cook for 6 minutes, stirring once halfway through. Remove beef from pot to clean plate or bowl.

2. With remaining oil in the pot (should be 1 tablespoon), add the onions, thyme, and garlic. Add in any remaining flour mixture as well and cook 2-3 minutes or until onions soften. Press "Cancel".

3. Stir in the broth and scrape up any browned bits on the bottom of the pot (for extra flavor). Add worcestershire sauce and bay leaves. Add the meat back into the pot, and put the lid on your pressure cooker, and lock it in place. Press the "Beef/Pork" button and press "Start." (35 minute pressure cooking time)

4. When cooking is finished, let the pressure release naturally by not touching any buttons for 10 minutes. Then, after 10 minutes, release any remaining pressure by pressing the steam release valve. When the indicator drops, it is safe to open the lid. Remove bay leaves. Serve with biscuits or mashed potatoes and a salad.

Nutrition Facts	Amount/serving	% Daily Value*	Amount/serving	% Daily Value*	
	Total Fat 19.5g	30%	Total Carbohydrates 18g	5%	* The percent Daily Value (DV) tells you how much a nutrient in a serving of food contributes to a daily diet. 2,000 calories a day is used for general nutrition advice.
6 servings	Saturated Fat 6.2g	30%	Dietary Fiber 3g	13%	
	Trans Fat 0.0g		Total Sugars 6g		
Calories 351 per serving	Cholesterol 85mg	28%			
	Sodium 529mg	23%	Protein 27g		
	Vitamin D 0mcg 0% · Calcium 70mg 7% · Iron 3mg 16% · Potassium 614mg 13%				

Macaroni and Cheese

PREP TIME: 2 MIN   PRESSURE COOKING TIME: 5 MIN   ADDITIONAL TIME: 10 MIN

SERVINGS: 6

Simple, easy, and delicious — that's how I would describe this recipe. My family would say, "Can you make that again?" I love serving it with cooked carrots and a salad. The result is a creamy pasta dish that everyone will love, and you will be amazed that it only took 5 minutes of pressure cooking time.

Ingredients

16 ounces dry elbow macaroni

2 tablespoons butter

4 cups water

½ teaspoon salt

12 ounces half and half or evaporated milk

8 ounces shredded sharp cheddar cheese

¼ cup shredded Parmesan cheese

Directions

1. Add macaroni, butter, water, and salt to your pressure cooker pot. Lock lid to seal. Press "Custom" and adjust time to 5 minutes.
2. When cooking time has finished, press the steam release button to release the pressure. Once the indicator drops, open the lid.
3. Stir in half and half and cheese until combined. Serve with salad.

Nutrition Facts	Amount/serving	% Daily Value*	Amount/serving	% Daily Value*	* The percent Daily Value (DV)
	Total Fat 23.5g	36%	**Total Carbohydrates** 60g	20%	tells you how much a nutrient in a serving of food contributes
6 servings	Saturated Fat 13.6g	68%	Dietary Fiber 2g	9%	to a daily diet. 2,000 calories a day is used for general
	Trans Fat 0.0g		Total Sugars 4g		nutrition advice.
Calories 552	**Cholesterol** 75mg	24%			
per serving	**Sodium** 546mg	23%	**Protein** 23g		
	Vitamin D 0mcg 0% · Calcium 399mg 39% · Iron 3mg 14% · Potassium 258mg 5%				

Simple Side Dish: Salad Mix & Match

Keep things simple by making the same type of side dish with all of these pressure cooking meals. Of course, you can incorporate variety with the flavors I share below, but there is no decision fatigue because you know what to put with each main dish — a salad!

Fall Harvest Salad
Spinach
Apples
Dried Cranberries
Walnuts
Poppyseed Dressing
Parmesan Cheese

Cobb Salad
Romaine Lettuce
Hard Cooked Eggs
Bacon Bits
Tomatoes
Avocado
Cheddar Cheese
Your Favorite Dressing

Caesar Salad
Iceberg or Romaine Lettuce
Croutons
Parmesan Cheese
Caesar Dressing

Southwest Salad
Romaine Lettuce
Tomatoes
Avocado
Black Beans
Cheddar Cheese
Tortilla Strips
Cilantro Lime Dressing

Asian Salad
Cabbage
Carrots
Green Onions
Chow Mein Noodles
Bell Pepper
Edamame
Asian Vinaigrette

Greek Salad
Romaine or Iceberg Lettuce
Cucumbers
Red Onions
Feta Cheese
Olives
Italian Vinaigrette

Simple Salad
Romaine Lettuce
Tomatoes
Carrots
Cucumbers
Shredded Cheese
Your favorite dressing

Your Favorite Salad

If you haven't already taken a moment to write out which of the recipes in this chapter you will incorporate in your menu map, do that here:

The Top 5 Meals I want to put into my menu map:

1.

2.

3.

4.

5.

This strategy is simple — which is the same as my cooking motto "KISS": Keep It Simple Sister! Pick the top five recipes you want to put into your menu map, note that the side dish is always salad for that extra boost of fiber, color, vitamins, and minerals, and then you can simply add a bowl of fruit and glass of milk. Easy.

If you want to stay awhile in the pressure cooker zone, you can master this cooking method before moving on to others. Pressure cooking is a cooking method that, once mastered, you will never go without. I have often said if I were heading to a deserted island with only one piece of cooking equipment, it would be my pressure cooker because of its versatility, its ease of use, and its speed. I hope you find those same benefits immediately when you are trying the recipes in this chapter!

Resources on my website:

- Find the specific pressure cooker I recommend with how-to videos.
- Watch me cook in my recipe videos where I share how to get started with pressure cooking.
- Other helpful tools I recommend.

CHAPTER FOUR

Air Fryer Recipes

A strong family has well–worn seats
at the dinner table.

~Unknown

You've made it through the menu mapping, you have already plotted your pressure cooking meals for the busiest days of the week, and perhaps you have even tried one of the meals. Yay for you! Look how far you are coming through this process. Just by going through this book and making a menu map, you are leaps ahead of where most people are. You should be super impressed with yourself.

Now is a great time to start talking to your friends about the progress you are making as well. You could become their savior just by sharing this process with them and save them so much time too. My goal is to simplify this as much as possible for you — forever — and to change how you think about meal planning. Let's dive into air frying. I like to think of my air fryer as an adult version of an Easy Bake Oven. I always wanted one of those when I was a kid because it would be my very own way to bake up a snack, or have my own "kitchen appliance." I never did get one, and it was a good thing I didn't. I bought one years later for my daughter and I was surprised to learn that the light bulb is what did the cooking, and just to bake a simple cookie took more than 35 minutes. That's way too long. Seriously, a light bulb to cook your food?

The only similarity with the air fryer and the Easy Bake Oven are the fact that they are compact. The main difference is in the way an air fryer cooks —

it is much more efficient and fast. Because of the compact area inside the air fryer, the hot air that is blown around by the powerful fan cooks and crisps food in an instant.

Because I was a company product tester for the air fryer I own, I really needed to learn it and be able to share my experiences with others. That was an intimidating feeling! I thought I had to get it right each time I made something, because the pressure was on to test multiple recipes and provide feedback for the company. I started with things that were simple and I knew my family would eat.

There was no better place to start than with chicken wings. This was significant because before the air fryer, I was pretty much anti-chicken wing — meaning I never once prepared them for my family in almost 20 years of cooking for them, and I also never ordered them if we went out to eat because I just didn't like that they were deep fried. But that all changed instantly when I made chicken wings in my air fryer. For two pounds of wings, I added only one tablespoon of oil (recipe in this chapter), and I tossed them with some seasonings. I put them on the grates inside the air fryer and let the machine do its thing.

I really didn't think they would come out as great as they did. I was surprised when I took my first bite of the air fryer chicken wing. There was a big crunch just as if I had bitten into a piece of crispy fried chicken at a restaurant — all from just minimal oil and seasonings! They were healthier and super easy to prepare. That's what I call a win-win!

Air frying helps you cook up meals you love with fewer calories and in less time. You are not drenching the foods you love in oil (like in a deep fryer); instead, you are letting the convection fan work to blow around the hot air to provide those same crispy results. You save time because of how quickly it cooks and that there is no preheating time involved, especially when you think of all those recipes that require preheating the oven. I also love roasting vegetables in the air fryer because they are done in a fraction of the time it would take to make them in the oven, with no preheating required. They get that caramelized texture and are so delicious with any meal. I often will roast them below the main protein I am making for dinner — like beneath the fish or chicken.

Top Tips for Using an Air Fryer (that has multiple trays and cooking rack positions):

1. When using two cooking trays, don't overcrowd the food on each tray. It's best to place one tray on the top rack and one on the middle. If you are using just one tray, just place it in the middle rack.

2. When half the cooking time has elapsed, flip flop the trays so their positions are opposite and all food gets evenly cooked.

3. To roast vegetables, place all vegetables in a large bowl and toss with ½ to 1 tablespoon oil and seasonings of your choice. Evenly divide the vegetables between the trays and select the roast setting. Time for roasting is anywhere between 4-24 minutes depending on the vegetable.

4. Pat your fish or chicken dry before adding seasonings.

5. Do not use foil inside the air fryer. It is not recommended as pieces can break off and blow into the heating element, overheat, and cause a fire.

6. When brushing or spraying the cooking trays with oil, it's best to use the actual oil to avoid the sticky residue that can develop with non-stick cooking sprays. That's why I recommend the kitchen spritzer (found on my website).

7. Wipe down the inside of the air fryer between cooking sessions to keep things working well. Just use a dishcloth with hot soapy water. You can also use a degreaser.

8. You can convert oven recipes to air fryer recipes really easily.

Here's how:

- Oven to air fryer: Reduce temperature of an oven recipe by 25 degrees and cut the cook time by 20%. Check food to evaluate doneness (use a meat thermometer when needed for proteins).
- Deep fryer to air fryer: Spritz food with oil before air frying, and rotate trays half way through cooking time.
- Skillet to air fryer: Place batter-coated or non battered food on a cooking tray and spritz with oil; follow recipe for timing instructions. Rotate trays half way through cooking time.
- Grill to air fryer: Place steak, fish, chicken, or pork in the air fryer and flip over half way through cooking time. Use a meat thermometer to check doneness.

Let's go back to the menu plan for this night of the week. The recipes I am including in this chapter are simple and easy, and will allow you to get the most out of your air fryer so you feel like it's really saving you energy. They are all very easy to combine with roasted vegetables (recipe also included in this chapter) to balance out the protein with the meal. The goal would be to have half of your plate be fruits/vegetables, while a quarter is the protein portion so you are getting all the extra nutrition you can. (The last quarter of the plate is for something grain-like — think brown rice, pasta, or whole grain bread).

Some helpful tools in this chapter include:

- Air Fryer with multiple Cooking Trays
- Kitchen Spritzer (for spritzing your own oil onto trays or food)
- Instant Read Food Thermometer (to test doneness of proteins)
- Nesting Coating Trays (to evenly coat proteins with a crunchy batter)

Barbecue Sriracha Chicken Wings

PREP TIME: 5 MIN   COOK TIME: 30 MIN   TOTAL TIME: 35 MIN

SERVINGS: 6

If your family loves wings, they will love this recipe! As I stated earlier in the chapter, they will crunch in your mouth after cooking thanks to that baking powder. They go well with roasted potato wedges.

Ingredients

2 dozen chicken wings or drumettes (about 3-4 pounds)

2 tablespoons canola oil

½ teaspoon each salt and black pepper

2 teaspoons baking powder

½ cup sweet barbecue sauce

1 tablespoon Asian-style hot sauce such as Sriracha

Directions

1. Pat wings dry with a paper towel. Combine wings, oil, salt, black pepper, and baking powder in a large mixing bowl and toss until evenly coated. Let stand for 5 minutes.

2. Spray the cooking trays with oil and transfer the wings to the two cooking trays inside the air fryer. Position trays on the top and middle racks.

3. Close the air fryer door, set to "Air Fry" setting, and adjust time to 30 minutes.

4. Meanwhile, in a separate smaller bowl, combine barbecue sauce and hot sauce.

5. When the wings are finished cooking (wings should reach 165 degrees), remove from the air fryer and brush sauce over the wings or serve on the side. Serve with roasted vegetables.

Nutrition Facts	Amount/serving	% Daily Value*	Amount/serving	% Daily Value*	
6 servings	**Total Fat** 6.4g	9%	**Total Carbohydrates** 10g	3%	* The percent Daily Value (DV) tells you how much a nutrient in a serving of food contributes to a daily diet. 2,000 calories a day is used for general nutrition advice.
	Saturated Fat 0.3g	1%	Dietary Fiber 0g	1%	
	Trans Fat 0.0g		Total Sugars 8g		
Calories 252 per serving	**Cholesterol** 0mg	0%			
	Sodium 553mg	24%	**Protein** 48g		
	Vitamin D 0mcg 0% · Calcium 9mg 0% · Iron 0mg 1% · Potassium 68mg 1%				

Crispy Chicken Tenders

PREP TIME: 5 MIN   COOK TIME: 10 MIN   TOTAL TIME: 15 MIN

SERVINGS: 4

I don't think I know a kid who doesn't like chicken nuggets — mine included. These are homemade, healthier, and very easy to make. The panko breadcrumbs provide the right texture, but feel free to swap in regular bread crumbs if you don't have panko on hand.

Ingredients

1½ cups panko bread crumbs

½ cup freshly grated Parmesan cheese

¼ teaspoon garlic powder

½ teaspoon Italian seasoning

¼ teaspoon each salt and black pepper

2 egg whites

1 tablespoon water

1 pound boneless, skinless chicken tenders

Directions

1. In a plastic coating tray, combine panko bread crumbs, cheese, and seasonings. In a separate plastic coating tray, add egg whites and water and whisk together.
2. Dip each chicken tender into egg mixture and then into bread crumb mixture.
3. Spray air fryer cooking grates with canola oil. Arrange chicken in a single layer on two different grates. Set to "Bake" for 10 minutes, or until the temperature reads 165 degrees. Serve with roasted vegetables (can be cooked at the same time in the air fryer).

Note — if you prefer plain boneless, skinless chicken breasts, just add your favorite seasoning and set to bake for 15 minutes or until temperature is at 165.

Nutrition Facts	Amount/serving	% Daily Value*	Amount/serving	% Daily Value*	
4 servings	**Total Fat** 8.6g	13%	**Total Carbohydrates** 14g	4%	* The percent Daily Value (DV) tells you how much a nutrient in a serving of food contributes to a daily diet. 2,000 calories a day is used for general nutrition advice.
	Saturated Fat 1.7g	8%	Dietary Fiber 2g	7%	
	Trans Fat 0.0g		Total Sugars 1g		
Calories 242 per serving	**Cholesterol** 7mg	2%			
	Sodium 361mg	15%	**Protein** 44g		
	Vitamin D 0mcg 0% · Calcium 128mg 12% · Iron 1mg 4% · Potassium 42mg 0%				

Crunchy Cod

PREP TIME: 5 MIN COOK TIME: 9 MIN TOTAL TIME: 14 MIN

SERVINGS: 4

This is one of my favorite ways to eat fish. It cooks quickly, is juicy and not dry, and has the perfect crunch on the top. You can swap out your favorite white fish in this recipe as needed.

Ingredients

4 fresh cod fillets (4–5 ounces each)

¼ cup mayonnaise

2 tablespoons butter, melted

½ cup whole wheat panko bread crumbs

½ teaspoon garlic powder

½ teaspoon dried parsley

¼ teaspoon salt

⅛ teaspoon black pepper

Directions

1. Pat cod dry with a paper towel. Brush top of cod fillet with mayonnaise. Mix butter with bread crumbs and seasonings. Lightly press bread crumb mixture onto tops of cod fillets.
2. Lightly spray air fryer cooking grates with canola oil. Arrange cod fillets so they are not touching each other. Place the grate on the top rack slot. Set the air fryer to "Roast" setting for 9 minutes. Serve with roasted vegetables (can be roasted below the cod).

Note — this recipe also makes fabulous fish tacos.
Just cut the fish into smaller bite size pieces (it should flake apart) after it's finished cooking and arrange into a tortilla with tomatoes, lettuce, and cilantro. Add a fruit salsa for a special zing. Just mix together 1 cup freshly diced peaches, mangos, or pineapple with ¼ cup diced onion, 1 minced jalapeno, juice of one lime, and minced fresh cilantro with a sprinkle of salt. Yum!

Nutrition Facts	Amount/serving	% Daily Value*	Amount/serving	% Daily Value*	
	Total Fat 8.6g	13%	**Total Carbohydrates** 4g	1%	* The percent Daily Value (DV) tells you how much a nutrient in a serving of food contributes to a daily diet. 2,000 calories a day is used for general nutrition advice.
	Saturated Fat 3.8g	18%	Dietary Fiber 1g	2%	
4 servings	Trans Fat 0.0g		Total Sugars 0g		
	Cholesterol 76mg	25%			
Calories 193 per serving	**Sodium** 275mg	11%	**Protein** 26g		
	Vitamin D 1mcg 12% · Calcium 24mg 2% · Iron 1mg 4% · Potassium 588mg 12%				

Hawaiian Coconut Shrimp

PREP TIME: 10 MIN   COOK TIME: 8 MIN   TOTAL TIME: 18 MIN

SERVINGS: 4

I had the best coconut shrimp in Hawaii from a food truck, and this recipe reminds me of that memory. Definitely prepare the sauce because it is the icing on the cake.

Ingredients

16 ounces large shrimp (31–35 count), peeled, deveined and tails on

½ teaspoon salt

½ teaspoon black pepper

¾ cup all-purpose flour

2 eggs

1 tablespoon milk

1 cup sweetened shredded coconut

¾ cup whole wheat panko breadcrumbs

3 tablespoons butter, melted

1 lime, zested

Sauce:

6 tablespoons peach or apricot preserves

3 tablespoons sweet Thai chili sauce

Directions

1. Pat shrimp dry with paper towels. In a medium bowl, add shrimp, salt, and pepper. Toss to evenly coat.
2. In a plastic coating tray, add flour.
3. In a second plastic coating tray, whisk eggs and milk together.
4. In a third plastic coating tray, combine coconut, bread crumbs, butter, and lime zest.
5. Dip each shrimp first into flour, secondly into the egg mixture, and thirdly into coconut mixture. Gently press to adhere the coating. Repeat with remaining shrimp.
6. Spray air fryer cooking trays with oil and divide shrimp evenly between two trays. Place shrimp around the outer edge of trays, leaving the center open. Place racks on the middle and lower racks of the air fryer. Select the "Bake" setting and adjust time to 8 minutes. Swap each rack half way through cooking time.
7. Meanwhile, mix together dipping sauce ingredients and microwave for 45 seconds. Serve as desired with suggestions above along with roasted vegetables. Serving options: Serve over cooked jasmine rice made with coconut milk, on a hoagie style bun with coleslaw, or on top of a salad.

Nutrition Facts	Amount/serving	% Daily Value*	Amount/serving	% Daily Value*	
4 servings	**Total Fat** 24.6g	37%	**Total Carbohydrates** 41g	13%	* The percent Daily Value (DV) tells you how much a nutrient in a serving of food contributes to a daily diet. 2,000 calories a day is used for general nutrition advice.
	Saturated Fat 13.5g	67%	Dietary Fiber 5g	21%	
	Trans Fat 0.0g		Total Sugars 11g		
Calories 465 per serving	**Cholesterol** 298mg	99%			
	Sodium 604mg	26%	**Protein** 33g		
	Vitamin D 1g 5% · Calcium 96mg 9% · Iron 3mg 14% · Potassium 504mg 10%				

Steak Kebabs

PREP TIME: 5 MIN   COOK TIME: 10 MIN   TOTAL TIME: 15 MIN

SERVINGS: 4

Using the air fryer to make these steak kebabs really cuts down the time it takes to cook them, and you also save the steak (how often has the steak fallen into the fire on the grill?). Feel free to swap out the steak for other styles of protein in this recipe too.

Ingredients

1 pound beef sirloin steak, cut into 1½ inch cubes

1 tablespoon garlic infused canola oil

1 tablespoon steak seasoning

1 red onion, wedged into 8 pieces

8 ounces baby bella mushrooms, halved

Directions

1. Add steak, oil, seasoning, onions, and mushrooms to a mixing bowl and toss to coat.
2. Carefully thread 3 pieces of meat and 5 vegetables on each skewer.
3. Place skewers into the air fryer and set to "Rotisserie" setting for 10 minutes or until beef reaches 145 degrees. Adjust time to 14 minutes if you like well done. Serve with mashed potatoes and crusty bread or a salad.

Note:If you swap out steak for chicken breasts, then alter the seasoning and vegetables. Set for 16-20 minutes of cook time on "Rotisserie" setting, or until temperature reaches 165 degrees.

Nutrition Facts	Amount/serving	% Daily Value*	Amount/serving	% Daily Value*	
	Total Fat 18.0g	27%	Total Carbohydrates 6g	1%	* The percent Daily Value (DV) tells you how much a nutrient in a serving of food contributes to a daily diet. 2,000 calories a day is used for general nutrition advice.
	Saturated Fat 6.3g	31%	Dietary Fiber 1g	5%	
4 servings	Trans Fat 0.0g		Total Sugars 3g		
	Cholesterol 85mg	28%			
Calories 285 per serving	Sodium 936mg	40%	Protein 25g		
	Vitamin D 0g 1% · Calcium 38mg 3% · Iron 2mg 10% · Potassium 621mg 13%				

*Reduce sodium by using a salt-free rub.

Rotisserie Pork Tenderloin

PREP TIME: 5 MIN   COOK TIME: 35 MIN   TOTAL TIME: 40 MIN

SERVINGS: 4

The first time I made this recipe, I was amazed at how juicy and tender the roast was and how little time it took to cook. I also like making my own rotisserie chicken in the same way. It saves so much money to make it yourself, and you get to control the sodium levels too.

Ingredients

1.5 pound pork roast (Hormel Always Tender is my favorite)

1 tablespoon canola oil

2-3 tablespoons smoky barbecue rub

Rotisserie chicken option: Swap out the pork for a 4 pound chicken and make your own rotisserie chicken at home, with an outer crispy skin and juicy meat inside. Follow the same instructions with brushing oil, and then tie the legs together with a 12 inch piece of cooking twine. Then tie the wings against the breasts with a 24 inch piece of cooking twine. Insert the spit through the legs where they are tied together and through the cavity, centering as able. Sprinkle chicken with your favorite seasoning. Cook for 45 minutes on "Rotisserie" setting or until temperature reaches 165 degrees.

Directions

1. Place pork tenderloin on a plastic cutting board. Brush with canola oil and season with barbecue rub, making sure to press seasoning into pork. Insert the rotisserie spit into the center of the pork roast. Tie cooking twine around the roast at 1-2 inch intervals. Slide the rotisserie forks onto both ends of the spit and into the food with the prongs facing inward. Tighten the screws to lock in place.

2. Insert the spit into the air fryer and align it into the rotisserie slot. Set to "Rotisserie" setting and adjust time to 35 minutes. Press the "rotation" button so pork spins during cooking. Pork should be 145 degrees when finished cooking. Let rest for 5 minutes on a cutting board to allow juices to redistribute. Serve with roasted vegetables (can be roasted under the pork if they fit) and mashed potatoes.

Note: This recipe could also be made into thinly sliced pork sandwiches with barbecue sauce for barbecue pork sandwiches, or served with a salad.

Nutrition Facts	Amount/serving	% Daily Value*	Amount/serving	% Daily Value*	
	Total Fat 7.2g	11%	Total Carbohydrates 3g	1%	* The percent Daily Value (DV) tells you how much a nutrient in a serving of food contributes to a daily diet. 2,000 calories a day is used for general nutrition advice.
4 servings	Saturated Fat 1.4g	7%	Dietary Fiber 0g	0%	
	Trans Fat 0.0g		Total Sugars 3g		
Calories **229** per serving	Cholesterol 111mg	36%			
	Sodium 190mg	8%	Protein 36g		
	Vitamin D 0mcg 3% · Calcium 12mg 1% · Iron 2mg 9% · Potassium 698mg 14%				

Pizza Stromboli

PREP TIME: 10 MIN   COOK TIME: 14 MIN   TOTAL TIME: 24 MIN

SERVINGS: 6

Another fast weeknight meal that tastes like you got it at a restaurant. This stromboli is customizable if you want to swap out the toppings.

Ingredients

1 package (13.8 ounces) refrigerated classic pizza dough

1 teaspoon Italian seasoning or pizza seasoning, divided

1 tablespoon canola oil

1 bell pepper, diced

1 onion, diced

3 ounces Italian turkey sausage crumbles, fully cooked

1 cup freshly grated Parmesan cheese

1 cup grated mozzarella cheese

Pizza sauce for dipping

Note: You can make barbecue chicken stromboli by swapping out the sausage crumbles and using barbecue seasoning in place of the Italian seasoning. Continue with the peppers and onions, and serve with barbecue sauce.

Directions

1. Unroll pizza dough onto a lightly floured surface. Roll into a 16x10-inch rectangle. Sprinkle seasoning over the dough.
2. Meanwhile, heat a small fry pan on medium heat on stove top. Add oil and gently cook the bell pepper and onion until softened. Remove from heat and let cool for 5 minutes.
3. Cut dough in half lengthwise so you have two 8x10 inch pieces. Layer the sausage crumbles, the bell pepper and onion, along with the cheeses.
4. Along short sides of dough, start rolling up jelly-roll style into a log and press ends to seal. Repeat with the other piece of dough. Cut 5 slits on top of each log. Sprinkle both with remaining Italian seasoning.
5. Spray one air fryer cooking tray with canola oil. Place both dough logs onto the tray and place on the bottom rack of the air fryer. Set to "Bake" setting for 14 minutes. Flip log over half way through cooking time. Serve with pizza sauce and salad or roasted vegetables.

Nutrition Facts		Amount/serving	% Daily Value*	Amount/serving	% Daily Value*	
		Total Fat 24.2g	37%	**Total Carbohydrates** 32g	10%	* The percent Daily Value (DV) tells you how much a nutrient in a serving of food contributes to a daily diet. 2,000 calories a day is used for general nutrition advice.
6 servings		Saturated Fat 6.3g	31%	Dietary Fiber 6g	22%	
		Trans Fat 0.1g		Total Sugars 5g		
Calories	**413**	**Cholesterol** 37mg	12%			
per serving		**Sodium** 706mg	30%	**Protein** 19g		
		Vitamin D 0mcg 1% · Calcium 357mg 35% · Iron 202mg 1123% · Potassium 559mg 11%				

Simple Side Dish:
Roasted Vegetables

Plan ½ cup vegetables per person so everyone gets a serving.

California Mix Roast Setting – 15 minutes – middle or lower rack	Garden Vegetables (Asparagus, Zucchini, Broccoli) Roast Setting – 8-10 minutes – middle or lower rack
Potatoes – Regular or Sweet Cut into 1 inch cubes Roast Setting – 15-20 minutes – middle or lower rack	Winter Squash Cut into 1 inch cubes Roast Setting – 15-20 minutes – middle or lower rack

What are the top five recipes you plan to implement right away in your menu map?

List them here:

1.

2.

3.

4.

5.

Now, add them to your menu map so that you can start to see the month of meals come together. These recipes will quickly become favorites in your family dinners, as they are simple, inexpensive to prepare, leave you feeling confident in the kitchen, and you will want to repeat them on a routine basis. That is the precise reason to make this menu map. There is no reason to have 52 different air fryer meals; instead, pick your top four or eight and make them every month or every other month on a rotating basis. It's like when you go to a restaurant and you order that same meal each time because you know it's good. It's the same at home – do not be afraid to simplify this process.

You now have two nights taken care of in your forever dinner plan. You are ready to implement and execute. Let's keep marching on to the next chapter!

Resources on my website:
- Find the specific air fryer I recommend with how-to videos.
- Watch me cook in my recipe videos where I share how to get started with air frying.
- Other helpful tools I recommend.

CHAPTER FIVE

Grill/Griddle Recipes

Family Recipe·
__2 cups of forgiveness + 1 gallon of friendship +__
__1 pinch of hope + 1 tablespoon of laughter__
__and endless love__
~Unknown

From pressure cooking to air frying, you are now equipped to handle dinner on nights where things are super busy, as well as when you just want some of those foods you love but healthier at the same time. You have made a plan for at least five pressure cooker meals for busy nights, and you have also made a list of five recipes from the air fryer when you are just out of energy to cook but want something healthy. Now let's talk about bringing the restaurant home to your own kitchen!

When my kids were born, I remember thinking to myself, I'm never taking them to a fast food restaurant. I wanted my kids to not even know what chicken nuggets or burgers and fries were unless they were made in our home. I quickly realized this was so unrealistic and an elitist mentality. Seriously, just because I was a dietitian, I thought I could keep them away from fast food? I know this stemmed from my work with my patients who had heart disease and from encouraging them to avoid higher fat and fried foods. I wanted to do the same with my family. With all the extra responsibilities that come along with having children such as youth sports, nightly homework, and wanting to spend time together, it's hard to avoid the fast food line. It quickly became overwhelming and I found myself running through the drive-through more times than I would like to count.

Enter copycat recipes — recipes that are inspired by our favorite restaurants featuring foods we love to order, but in a healthier way. Not only are they healthier, but they are also much more wallet-friendly too.

Think about all the places you like to dine in. What do they have in common? Do you tend to like a certain style of food? Perhaps it's hibachi grill or Latin flavors. Perhaps it's traditional burgers of all kinds. Or maybe it's diner food like pancakes and omelettes and French toast. Maybe it's that favorite sandwich and soup restaurant you love that makes the best panini sandwiches. Did you know you can make them all at home in less time and healthier with a smart grill?

A smart grill is basically an appliance that acts not only as a griddle, but also a grill. It has plates that can be interchanged for other types of cooking — including grill plates, griddle plates, and even waffle plates. This gives you ultimate versatility. It's perfect for burger night, panini night, and nights where you want to grill shrimp or chicken but you don't actually want to go outside and grill shrimp or chicken. It's amazing for breakfast for dinner because you can cook so many servings at once, allowing you more time around the table with your family actually eating together.

To help you assess what really happens when you go out to eat, run through the drive-through, or go to your favorite sit down spot, make a quick list of the top five places you tend to go to when life is busy:

1.

2.

3.

4.

5.

Now, make a quick list of the top food item you or your family members love to order from each of those places:

1.

2.

3.

4.

5.

If you are seeing a pattern in where you like to eat out and what foods you choose when you eat out, you can probably replicate some of those meals in a healthier way at home at a fraction of the cost.

This is also the perfect time to get your family involved with cooking; the recipes in this chapter can be personalized a bit because of the "bar style" recipes. For example, the panini bar — simply laying out all the ingredients to choose from including breads, cheeses, meats, veggies, and sauces, perhaps even fruit like apples or pears, allows everyone in the house to be really creative and come up with their own favorite recipe! It's as if they are the chef in the restaurant, and this provides a great opportunity to make dinner a fun family event.

If you don't have a smart grill, you can use a nonstick griddle or grill pan as an alternative option. Just look for a large grill pan that has grilling slats so you get grill marks, and a large flat griddle so you have a lot of space to cook. However, smart grills offer some nice time savings as they can cook both from the top and the bottom plates, meaning foods cook twice as fast. Also, it can be laid flat to have a more open area for cooking things like breakfast for dinner. I also love the preset features that allow you to set the time and the temperature and it will cook for you. In the smart grill I have, you can also insert the probe into the meat you are preparing and set the temperature you want the probe to get to, and it will stop cooking once it reaches that temperature.

Here are my top five tips for using the smart grill, such as the Deluxe Electric Grill and Griddle that I recommend:

1. Lay out all the ingredients while you are preheating the grill/griddle. Depending on how hot you are setting the temperature, it can take two to five minutes to preheat. Use that time to grab all your ingredients and lay everything out for easy meal prep. Things will go much faster and be more efficient for you.
2. Use the griddle plates for eggs, quesadillas, crunch wraps, sandwiches, French toast, pancakes, and even shrimp and vegetables.
3. Use the grill plates for anything you want to have grill marks on — panini sandwiches, chicken, steak, burgers, pork chops, quesadillas, and more.
4. Use the waffle plates for making waffles, waffle sandwiches, waffle quesadillas, waffle pizzas, and even fun breakfasts like flattened cinnamon rolls.
5. Be sure you are using a food thermometer for food safety. Here's a quick list of temperatures:
    a. Ground meats: 160 degrees
    b. Chicken/turkey: 165 degrees
    c. Beef/lamb: 135 degrees (medium rare), 155 degrees (medium well)
    d. Fish: 145 degrees
    e. Pork: 145 degrees (medium), 160 degrees (well-done)

Some helpful tools in this chapter include:

- Deluxe Electric Grill & Griddle (or another option is to use a grill pan with press and flat griddle pan)
- Kitchen Spritzer (for spritzing your own oil onto trays or food)
- Instant Read Food Thermometer (to test doneness of proteins)
- Blender for smoothie making

Panini Night

PREP TIME: 5 MIN   COOK TIME: 5 MIN   TOTAL TIME: 10 MIN

SERVINGS: AS MANY AS YOU'D LIKE

When I don't have a solid plan for dinner, this is the recipe that I run to because it's quick, easy, and still makes me look like I have it together (even when I don't)! Everyone in the family can put their spin on their sandwich, and with a smart grill, you can make multiple sandwiches in 2 minutes and 30 seconds!

Ingredients

2 ounces thinly sliced turkey, ham, chicken, or roast beef

1 slice of cheese: cheddar, monterey jack, mozzarella, swiss, provolone

2 slices of bread: Italian, sourdough, rye, whole wheat, ciabatta

¼ to ½ cup thinly sliced vegetables or fruits such as onions, peppers, tomatoes, apples, or pears

Layering vegetables: spinach, arugula, or lettuce

Sauce: cranberry sauce, pesto sauce, barbecue sauce, mayonnaise, mustard

Extras: bacon, avocado, roasted bell peppers

Directions

1. Build your panini by placing meat and cheese on one side of the bread. On the other side, slather sauce, and add vegetables and extras. Put the sandwich together.

2. Set the smart grill to the "Panini" setting. (Alternatively, preheat a grill/griddle pan over medium heat for 2-3 minutes.) Brush the sandwich sides with melted butter, place on a grill pan, and close the top of the grill (or press the sandwich with pressure) for 2-3 minutes. (If not using a smart grill you will need to flip each sandwich). Serve with a smoothie.

Suggestions for combinations:
- Turkey, Provolone Cheese, and Cranberry Mayo
- Ham, Swiss Cheese, and Tomato
- Chicken, Pesto, and Mozzarella Cheese
- Turkey, Bacon, and Avocado with Cheddar
- Roast Beef, Peppers, Onions, and Cheddar

Nutrition Facts	Amount/serving	% Daily Value*	Amount/serving	% Daily Value*	
1 servings	**Total Fat** 13.2g	20%	**Total Carbohydrates** 53g	17%	* The percent Daily Value (DV) tells you how much a nutrient in a serving of food contributes to a daily diet. 2,000 calories a day is used for general nutrition advice.
	Saturated Fat 5.1g	25%	Dietary Fiber 7g	27%	
	Trans Fat 0.0g		Total Sugars 7g		
Calories **458** per serving	**Cholesterol** 65mg	21%			
	Sodium 961mg	41%	**Protein** 30g		
	Vitamin D 0mcg 0% · Calcium 55mg 5% · Iron 3mg 17% · Potassium 437mg 9%				

Smashed Slider Bar Night

PREP TIME: 5 MIN   COOK TIME: 5 MIN   TOTAL TIME: 10 MIN

SERVINGS: 6

A top favorite for my kids has always been burgers. This recipe is so simple and cooks quickly thanks to the size of the patty. Lay out the toppings and let everyone do their thing. You can even pop some French fries in the air fryer while the burgers are cooking!

Ingredients

1 pound lean ground beef

1 medium onion, finely diced

½ teaspoon salt

½ teaspoon pepper

12 slider buns, halved

Toppings: Lettuce, tomato slices, ketchup, mustard, pickles

Directions

1. Set the smart grill with grill plates inserted to the "Grill" setting to start preheating.
2. In a large bowl, mix together beef, onion, and salt and pepper. Form into 12 golf-ball sized meatballs.
3. Once the smart grill is heated, add meatballs to the griddle and smash them very flat by closing the lid to the smart grill (alternatively, preheat a cast iron skillet and smash each meatball with a metal spatula). Cook for 2-3 minutes on a smart grill or until the temperature of the beef reaches 160 degrees.
4. Once the patty is finished cooking, place the top half of the bun on top of the patty and let steam for 1 minute. Remove from the grill and serve with toppings and remaining bun. Serve with a smoothie.

Nutrition Facts	Amount/serving	% Daily Value*	Amount/serving	% Daily Value*	
	Total Fat 13.7g	21%	**Total Carbohydrates** 41g	13%	* The percent Daily Value (DV) tells you how much a nutrient in a serving of food contributes to a daily diet. 2,000 calories a day is used for general nutrition advice.
6 servings	Saturated Fat 4.5g	22%	Dietary Fiber 5g	18%	
	Trans Fat 0.4g		Total Sugars 5g		
Calories 400	**Cholesterol** 66mg	22%			
per serving	**Sodium** 562mg	24%	**Protein** 28g		
	Vitamin D 0mcg 0% · Calcium 21mg 2% · Iron 2mg 11% · Potassium 422mg 8%				

French Toast for Dinner

PREP TIME: 5 MIN   COOK TIME: 5 MIN   TOTAL TIME: 10 MIN

SERVINGS: 4

This is a top favorite whether I make it for dinner or for breakfast. It's simple, easy, and can be served with fruit, eggs, and turkey sausage for staying power. Plus any leftovers are great for breakfast the next day!

Ingredients

3 eggs

½ cup milk

½ teaspoon vanilla extract

1 teaspoon sugar

¼ teaspoon salt

1 tablespoon butter

8 slices of thick cut bread like brioche, texas toast, or French baguette

Directions

1. Set the smart grill to a flat, open position with griddle plates inserted and select "Griddle" setting to start preheating. (Alternatively, preheat a griddle pan over medium heat for 2-3 minutes.)
2. Meanwhile, whisk the eggs and milk with vanilla, sugar and salt in a shallow coating tray. Dip bread one slice at a time into egg mixture, coating both sides, and place on the preheated griddle.
3. Cook until golden brown, about 90 seconds per side. Flip and repeat for another 30-60 seconds. Serve with fresh cut berries, homemade whipped cream, turkey sausage, scrambled eggs, and a smoothie.

Nutrition Facts	Amount/serving	% Daily Value*	Amount/serving	% Daily Value*	
4 servings	Total Fat 8.8g	13%	Total Carbohydrates 32g	10%	* The percent Daily Value (DV) tells you how much a nutrient in a serving of food contributes to a daily diet. 2,000 calories a day is used for general nutrition advice.
	Saturated Fat 3.3g	16%	Dietary Fiber 1g	2%	
	Trans Fat 0.0g		Total Sugars 8g		
Calories 254 per serving	Cholesterol 148mg	49%			
	Sodium 610mg	26%	Protein 11g		
	Vitamin D 1mcg 7% · Calcium 78mg 7% · Iron 2mg 11% · Potassium 52mg 1%				

Quesadilla Night

PREP TIME: 5 MIN   COOK TIME: 5 MIN   TOTAL TIME: 10 MIN

SERVINGS: 8

If you tend to go to your favorite Mexican restaurant, then you will love how easy this recipe will be to make at home! It's one of our favorites and you can customize the flavors to what each member of the family likes just by having them build their own quesadilla.

Ingredients

8 tablespoons butter with canola oil (from tub in refrigerated section in grocery store)

2 cups cooked diced chicken, seasoned with reduced sodium taco seasoning

1 pound ground beef, cooked, seasoned with reduced sodium taco seasoning

½ cup reduced-sodium black beans, drained and rinsed

½ cup refried beans

1 bell pepper, thinly sliced

2 tomatoes, diced

4 ounce can green chiles, drained

1 yellow onion, diced

4 cups cheddar cheese, Monterey Jack cheese, or Colby Jack cheese

Fresh cilantro, minced

8 - 8-inch flour tortillas

Directions

1. Set the smart grill to a flat, open position with griddle plates inserted and select "Griddle" setting to start preheating. (Alternatively, use grill plates if you want grill marks).

2. Place all ingredients into separate small bowls. Butter one side of the tortilla, fill half of the unbuttered side of the tortilla with desired toppings and sprinkle cheese over half the tortilla. Repeat with remaining tortillas.

3. Working with two tortillas at a time, place the tortilla with toppings onto the griddle plate, buttered side down. Fold in half and close the smart grill to allow for cooking on both sides at once. Cook for 2-3 minutes, or until the cheese starts to melt. Repeat with remaining tortillas. Cut in wedges to serve. Serve with a smoothie.

Nutrition Facts	Amount/serving	% Daily Value*	Amount/serving	% Daily Value*	
	Total Fat 28.8g	44%	**Total Carbohydrates** 26g	8%	* The percent Daily Value (DV) tells you how much a nutrient in a serving of food contributes to a daily diet. 2,000 calories a day is used for general nutrition advice.
8 servings	Saturated Fat 16.4g	82%	Dietary Fiber 5g	18%	
	Trans Fat 0.0g		Total Sugars 4g		
Calories 458 per serving	**Cholesterol** 98mg	32%			
	Sodium 616mg	26%	**Protein** 27g		
Vitamin D 0mcg 2% · Calcium 354mg 35% · Iron 153mg 851% · Potassium 251mg 5%					

Note: Make the chicken and ground beef in advance so this recipe goes even faster for you.

Ginger Brown Sugar Glazed Salmon

PREP TIME: 5 MIN   COOK TIME: 8-10 MIN   TOTAL TIME: 13-15 MIN

SERVINGS: 4

This recipe comes from the time when I was working as a supermarket dietitian and I was doing cooking classes for customers. It always got rave reviews! When I made it at home for my family, they loved the flavors too. The sauce is what makes this recipe shine.

Ingredients

2 tablespoons brown sugar

2 teaspoons dijon mustard

2 teaspoons reduced sodium soy sauce

½ teaspoon ground ginger

Black pepper, to taste

4 (4 ounces each) salmon fillets

Sesame seeds

Directions

1. Preheat the grill/griddle to "Grill" setting. (Alternatively, preheat a grill pan over medium high heat for 2-3 minutes.)
2. In a small bowl, combine brown sugar, mustard, soy sauce, and ginger.
3. Season salmon to taste with black pepper.
4. Place salmon skin side up onto the grill pan. Let cook for 3-4 minutes. Then, flip and brush sauce over top of salmon, cooking 3-4 minutes more or until temperature reaches 145 degrees. Sprinkle with sesame seeds as desired. Serve with cooked rice or mashed potatoes, vegetables and a smoothie.

Nutrition Facts	Amount/serving	% Daily Value*	Amount/serving	% Daily Value*	
4 servings	**Total Fat** 14.8g	22%	**Total Carbohydrates** 2g	0%	* The percent Daily Value (DV) tells you how much a nutrient in a serving of food contributes to a daily diet. 2,000 calories a day is used for general nutrition advice.
	Saturated Fat 4.4g	21%	Dietary Fiber 0g	0%	
	Trans Fat 0.0g		Total Sugars 1g		
Calories **267** per serving	**Cholesterol** 71mg	23%			
	Sodium 230mg	10%	**Protein** 28g		
	Vitamin D 0g 0% · Calcium 38mg 3% · Iron 0mg 2% · Potassium 563mg 11%				

Chicken Fajitas

PREP TIME: 5 MIN   COOK TIME: 6 MIN   TOTAL TIME: 11 MIN

SERVINGS: 6

If you love taco night, then this will be the next level. Of course you can always make tacos, but to change things up, making this fast chicken fajita recipe will replicate that favorite Mexican restaurant that you may find yourself at. It's faster and healthier too!

Ingredients

2 green or red bell peppers, thinly sliced

2 medium yellow onions, thinly sliced

2 garlic cloves, pressed

1 tablespoon canola oil

1 ½ pounds boneless, skinless chicken breast tenderloins

2 tablespoons chipotle rub or chicken fajita seasoning (reduced-sodium preferred)

12 (6-inch) flour tortillas

½ cup nonfat plain Greek yogurt

1-½ cups shredded cheddar cheese

½ cup salsa

1 cup refried beans

1 bunch fresh cilantro

Directions

1. Set the grill to a flat, open position with grill plates inserted and select "grill" setting to start preheating.

2. Meanwhile, toss bell peppers, onions, and garlic in canola oil in a large bowl. Once the grill is preheated, pour vegetables onto one side of the hot grill plate. Use the same bowl to toss chicken and seasoning together and add to the other grill plate. Cook for 5-6 minutes, flipping with tongs once, until chicken reaches 165 degrees.

3. Using a clean bowl, remove chicken and vegetables from the grill and quickly cut with Salad Chopper or shred with two forks.

4. To make the fajitas, add chicken and vegetables to a tortilla, topped with plain yogurt, cheese, salsa, refried beans, and fresh cilantro. Serve with a smoothie.

Nutrition Facts	Amount/serving	% Daily Value*	Amount/serving	% Daily Value*	
6 servings	Total Fat 17.2g	26%	Total Carbohydrates 57g	18%	* The percent Daily Value (DV) tells you how much a nutrient in a serving of food contributes to a daily diet. 2,000 calories a day is used for general nutrition advice.
	Saturated Fat 7.2g	36%	Dietary Fiber 10g	40%	
	Trans Fat 0.0g		Total Sugars 9g		
Calories **545** per serving	Cholesterol 21mg	7%			
	Sodium 872mg	37%	Protein 54g		
	Vitamin D 0mcg 0% · Calcium 495mg 49% · Iron 403mg 2237% · Potassium 653mg 13%				

*Nutrition facts include all toppings.

Simple Side Dish: Smoothie Maker

This is the best way to get extra fruit in for the day, and we make smoothies frequently to boost nutrition. They are easy, fast and delicious!

Per one 12 ounce smoothie, pick 1 cup of frozen or fresh fruit below (if picking fresh, add ice to smoothie): Strawberries Blueberries Blackberries Pineapple Mango Peaches Apples Pears + Add ½ banana per smoothie	Add ¼ cup greek yogurt +½ cup of one of the below liquids: Milk or milk alternative Apple juice Orange juice Fruit juice puree (found in refrigerated section)

Which five recipes are you going to include on your menu map?

List them here:

1.

2.

3.

4.

5.

We are more than halfway through the week! That means you are more than 50% finished with your forever dinner plan! There are just two more nights to go, and these are fun ones too. I hope you are finding this as fun as I am; I am enjoying helping you simplify mealtime!

Resources on my website:

- Find the specific smart grill I recommend with how-to videos.
- Watch me cook in my recipe videos where I share how to get started with indoor grilling and griddling.
- Other helpful tools I recommend.

CHAPTER SIX

One Pot Recipes

Some of the most important conversations I have had have occurred at the family dinner table.

~Bob Ehrlich

We have gone through a lot of scenarios already. Busy nights get the pressure cooker. Nights when you want a healthy meal but you don't want to heat up the oven, get the air fryer meals. Instead of the drive-through, the smart grill takes care of dinner. And now we are at the point of making one pot/one pan meals which are huge clean up savers! But before you move forward, be sure you have used your menu map to plot out your pressure cooker meal night with the recipes you want to include, as well as the air fryer night and the grill/griddle night. If you have done that already, you are really starting to see things come together and these last couple of chapters will be a piece of cake. Remember, bite-sized pieces of bacon are easier to digest than the whole hog!

Have you had a day like this? It's Thursday night and we have been going, going, going all week from tennis meets to dance practice to work meetings that run late. And while the week started off great with quick and easy meals, the clean up kind of sneaks up on me. I have every intention to keep the kitchen tidy; I put all the dishes from Sunday and Monday into the dishwasher and start it. But it takes until Thursday to empty it out — the night I really don't want to spend hours in the kitchen cleaning up. Does that ever happen to you? Enter one pot/one pan meals.

The first time I made the Zesty Pasta Skillet in the dutch oven was the day that I realized I loved one pot meals. It started with sautéing the vegetables, adding the ground beef, and then the seasonings. Then, I simply added the sauce, the pasta, and the water and less than ten minutes later, dinner was done. And guess what — I didn't have to get out multiple pots in order for this delicious dinner to happen. Nor did I have to drain the pasta. It's all in one pot.

The best pots to use for one pot meal night are ones that can easily go from stove to oven without having to transfer into a different pan.

Here are some examples:

Enameled Cast Iron

This type of pot is glazed cast iron, meaning you have a super smooth surface on the inside that allows for easy clean up once you're done cooking. It holds heat very well, meaning you don't need to cook on high heat. Plus, the cleanup is so easy, as this is the only type of cast iron that can go in the dishwasher! Generally you can use this type of cookware in the oven and on the stovetop, meaning if you start a dish on the stove top and need to transfer it to the oven to melt the cheese, you can do that without changing pots. My favorite size is the dutch oven.

Cast Iron

When you want your recipes to have that even browned look to them and also be able to transfer from stove top to oven, this is a great choice. Not only that, it can also go from the grill to over the fire pit. It also holds heat very well, meaning you do not want to cook over high heat or your foods will burn very quickly. Instead, low to medium heat is all that is needed. To clean this type of cookware, you simply use hot water and a scraper to remove bits of food and dry immediately to prevent rust.

High Quality Non-Stick Cookware

This type of cookware is perfect for foods that generally tend to stick, because those foods like eggs, pancakes, and more won't stick at all. Look for high quality non-stick cookware that is made from POFA-free (POFA is a chemical associated with teflon coatings) material and can go in the dishwasher for easy cleanup. Because it's non-stick, it also means having to use less oil. It's healthier all around!

Stainless Steel Non-Stick Cookware

This type of cookware is great for stir-frying and getting the perfect sear on your food. You can sear on the stovetop and then transfer the dish into the oven to finish cooking, just like restaurants do. The important feature here is that it isn't just stainless steel, it also has a nonstick webbing inside the pan that makes it super easy to clean up. So you get the benefits from both — searing with stainless and easy clean up from being nonstick.

Hight Quality Sheet Pans

I can't share enough about sheet pan meals as well. These are meals where you pick a protein and two or more vegetables, drizzle some olive oil and some seasonings over the top, and you have yourself a sheet pan dinner that's generally done in less than 25 minutes. The key to sheet pan dinners is having the right heavy duty grade pan that can withstand temperatures up to 450 degrees and has a nonstick surface which makes for super easy clean up. Want to see my favorite? Check my website for the one I love, as well as recipe videos on mix and match sheet pan suppers to help inspire you to new ideas!

Besides good cookware, other helpful tools in this chapter include:
- Mix & Chop (for crumbling and cooking ground beef)
- A stainless steel, non-stick wok

Barbecues

PREP TIME: 5 MIN   COOK TIME: 10 MIN   TOTAL TIME: 15 MIN

SERVINGS: 4

This is a family favorite from long ago. I grew up with this recipe and now make it for my family, and they love it too. Some may call them sloppy joes, but we always called them barbecues. Serve these sandwiches with baked beans and potato salad.

Ingredients

1 pound lean ground beef

½ medium onion, diced

1 (10.5 ounce) can chicken gumbo (reduced sodium if available)

3 tablespoons ketchup

2 tablespoons mustard

2 tablespoons packed brown sugar

8 whole wheat hamburger buns

Directions

1. In a skillet over medium heat, add ground beef and onion. Cook and crumble ground beef 3-4 minutes or until beef reaches 160 degrees.
2. Add gumbo, ketchup, mustard, and brown sugar. Stir and simmer on low for 10 minutes. Serve on whole wheat hamburger buns with a side dish of baked beans and potato salad. Serve with additional snacking vegetables.

Nutrition Facts	Amount/serving	% Daily Value*	Amount/serving	% Daily Value*	
	Total Fat 20.6g	31%	**Total Carbohydrates** 56g	18%	* The percent Daily Value (DV) tells you how much a nutrient in a serving of food contributes to a daily diet. 2,000 calories a day is used for general nutrition advice.
4 servings	Saturated Fat 6.9g	34%	Dietary Fiber 6g	23%	
	Trans Fat 0.6g		Total Sugars 16g		
Calories 569 per serving	**Cholesterol** 102mg	34%			
	Sodium 1131mg	49%	**Protein** 40g		
	Vitamin D 0mcg 0% · Calcium 52mg 5% · Iron 4mg 20% · Potassium 632mg 13%				

*Nutrition facts with regular canned soup (not low sodium)

General Tso Chicken and Vegetable Stir Fry

PREP TIME: 15 MIN COOK TIME: 16 MIN TOTAL TIME: 31 MIN

SERVINGS: 4

The first time I made this recipe, it seemed like we were eating at one of those Chinese restaurants at the mall, but much healthier. It got rave reviews the first time and continues to do so. You can swap out the vegetables to those you have on hand if you like, but these are tried and true.

Ingredients

Sauce:

¼ cup honey

⅓ cup low sodium soy sauce

1 ½ tablespoons Sriracha sauce

2 garlic cloves, pressed

Chicken:

1 pound chicken breasts

¼ cup corn starch

2 tablespoons canola oil

Vegetables:

1 yellow onion, thinly sliced

1 medium zucchini, thinly sliced

2 cups pre-shredded cabbage and carrot coleslaw mix

1 green bell pepper, thinly sliced

1 red bell pepper, thinly sliced

1 medium carrot, thinly sliced

Directions

1. For the sauce, mix honey, soy sauce, Sriracha, and pressed garlic in a small bowl.
2. Cut chicken breasts into diced pieces, about 1 inch square. Place chicken into a large bowl and sprinkle with cornstarch plus 1 tablespoon of sauce from step 1.
3. Heat oil in a large skillet or wok for 3-5 minutes. Add chicken to wok and cook, without stirring, for 3 minutes. Then stir for another 2-3 minutes until the chicken is evenly browned. Remove from the pan.
4. Add remaining tablespoon of oil and all of the vegetables to the pan. Stir-fry for 3 minutes or until lightly softened. Stir and cook for 2 minutes longer.
5. Add chicken back to pan along with remaining sauce and cook for 3 minutes, or until all vegetables are crisp-tender and sauce is reduced. Serve over rice. Serve with additional snacking vegetables.

Serving: Serve with cooked white jasmine rice (2 cups of raw rice cooked in 3 cups of water).

Nutrition Facts	Amount/serving	% Daily Value*	Amount/serving	% Daily Value*	
	Total Fat 5.8g	8%	**Total Carbohydrates** 32g	10%	* The percent Daily Value (DV) tells you how much a nutrient in a serving of food contributes to a daily diet. 2,000 calories a day is used for general nutrition advice.
6 servings	Saturated Fat 0.4g	1%	Dietary Fiber 5g	19%	
	Trans Fat 0.0g		Total Sugars 17g		
	Cholesterol 0mg	0%			
Calories 259 per serving	**Sodium** 658mg	28%	**Protein** 26g		
	Vitamin D 0mcg 0% · Calcium 51mg 5% · Iron 400mg 2224% · Potassium 422mg 8%				

Chicken Pot Pie

PREP TIME: 10 MIN   COOK TIME: 35 MIN   TOTAL TIME: 45 MIN

SERVINGS: 6

This is comfort food at its best, and it is less calories because you're only using only one pie crust. I made this recipe easier for you because you start it on the stovetop and, without having to transfer the filling to another dish, you layer the top pie crust over the filling and put the whole pan into the oven. Be sure to use an oven-safe pan that goes from stove to oven!

Ingredients

5 tablespoons butter

⅓ cup diced onion

5 tablespoons all-purpose flour

½ teaspoon salt

¼ teaspoon pepper

14 ounces reduced sodium chicken broth

½ cup fat-free milk

2 cups shredded or diced cooked chicken

2-½ cups mixed frozen vegetables (potatoes, green beans, corn, and carrots)

½ (14.1 ounce) package refrigerated pie crust

Directions

1. Preheat the oven to 425 degrees. In a large oven-safe skillet over medium heat, add butter and onion. Cook and stir for 2 minutes or until onion is slightly softened. Sprinkle in flour, salt and pepper. Stir until flour starts to bubble, about 1-2 minutes.

2. Add broth and milk and whisk until bubbly and thickened.

3. Stir in chicken and vegetables. Remove from heat.

4. Unroll refrigerated pie crust and lay over the top of filling, pressing in to resemble a pie. Cut slits evenly to vent. Bake for 20 minutes at 425. Reduce heat to 350 and bake another 15 minutes, until the top is evenly browned and the filling is bubbling. Serve with additional snacking vegetables.

Nutrition Facts	Amount/serving	% Daily Value*	Amount/serving	% Daily Value*	
	Total Fat 5.8g	8%	**Total Carbohydrates** 32g	10%	* The percent Daily Value (DV) tells you how much a nutrient in a serving of food contributes to a daily diet. 2,000 calories a day is used for general nutrition advice.
6 servings	Saturated Fat 0.4g	1%	Dietary Fiber 5g	19%	
	Trans Fat 0.0g		Total Sugars 17g		
Calories 259	**Cholesterol** 0mg	0%			
per serving	**Sodium** 658mg	28%	**Protein** 26g		

Vitamin D 0mcg 0% · Calcium 51mg 5% · Iron 400mg 2224% · Potassium 422mg 8%

Tater Tot Casserole

PREP TIME: 10 MIN   COOK TIME: 30 MIN   TOTAL TIME: 40 MIN

SERVINGS: 6

A Minnesota staple, this recipe has been a top favorite for years. I started making it when my kids were little and it's always a winner! It's simple, easy, and in this recipe it goes from stove to oven in one pot.

Ingredients

1 pound lean ground beef

½ small yellow onion, diced

2 cups frozen green beans

1 (10 ounce) can reduced-sodium cream of mushroom soup

½ teaspoon black pepper

1 cup shredded cheddar cheese

½ (32 ounce) bag of mini tater tots

Directions

1. Preheat the oven to 350 degrees. Cook and crumble ground beef with onion in a large, oven-safe, nonstick skillet or cast iron pan over medium heat until meat is browned or reaches a temperature of 160 degrees.

2. Layer green beans over meat mixture and top with cream of mushroom soup. Sprinkle black pepper and cheese over top. Layer tater tots in organized fashion over the entire mixture.

3. Place the oven-safe pan in the oven and bake for 30 minutes. Serve with additional snacking vegetables.

Nutrition Facts	Amount/serving	% Daily Value*	Amount/serving	% Daily Value*	
6 servings	**Total Fat** 17.5g	26%	**Total Carbohydrates** 21g	7%	* The percent Daily Value (DV) tells you how much a nutrient in a serving of food contributes to a daily diet. 2,000 calories a day is used for general nutrition advice.
	Saturated Fat 7.4g	36%	Dietary Fiber 3g	10%	
	Trans Fat 0.4g		Total Sugars 3g		
Calories 347 per serving	**Cholesterol** 81mg	26%			
	Sodium 340mg	14%	**Protein** 26g		
	Vitamin D 0mcg 0% · Calcium 141mg 14% · Iron 3mg 18% · Potassium 725mg 15%				

Zesty Pasta Skillet

PREP TIME: 14 MIN   COOK TIME: 10 MIN   TOTAL TIME: 24 MIN

SERVINGS: 6

Put this on your menu map immediately — it will be a go-to favorite for years to come! You can swap out the style of pasta to change things up and even add a vegetable or two if you like.

Ingredients

1 tablespoon canola oil

1 medium yellow onion, diced

1 pound ground turkey sausage, Italian variety

1 garlic clove, pressed

1 (28 ounce) can reduced-sodium crushed tomatoes, undrained

1 (8 ounce) can tomato sauce

2 tablespoons tomato paste

1 tablespoon Italian Seasoning

3 cups water

16 ounces of penne pasta, uncooked

1 cup shredded mozzarella cheese

½ cup shredded parmesan cheese

Directions

1. Preheat the oven to 475 degrees. Heat oil in an oven-safe dutch oven for 3 minutes over medium heat. Add onion, turkey sausage, and garlic to the pot and cook for 5-6 minutes or until turkey sausage is no longer pink and reaches a temperature of 165 degrees.

2. Add diced tomatoes, tomato sauce, tomato paste, and Italian seasoning and simmer for another 5 minutes, stirring occasionally.

3. Add water and pasta and cook for 10 minutes or until pasta is al dente (it will finish cooking in the oven). Remove from heat and sprinkle cheeses over the top. Bake uncovered until the cheese is melted, about 5 minutes. Serve with snacking vegetables.

Nutrition Facts	Amount/serving	% Daily Value*	Amount/serving	% Daily Value*	
6 servings	**Total Fat** 14.6g	22%	**Total Carbohydrates** 69g	23%	* The percent Daily Value (DV) tells you how much a nutrient in a serving of food contributes to a daily diet. 2,000 calories a day is used for general nutrition advice.
	Saturated Fat 4.9g	24%	Dietary Fiber 5g	21%	
	Trans Fat 0.3g		Total Sugars 7g		
Calories **549** per serving	**Cholesterol** 74mg	24%			
	Sodium 708mg	30%	**Protein** 33g		
	Vitamin D 0mcg 0% · Calcium 283mg 28% · Iron 4mg 20% · Potassium 754mg 16%				

California Chicken and Rice Casserole

PREP TIME: 7 MIN   COOK TIME: 30 MIN   TOTAL TIME: 37 MIN

SERVINGS: 4

This recipe is inspired by one my mom made while I was growing up. She continues to bring it for potlucks. It's another comfort food style meal that is just right on a cool night.

Ingredients

4 tablespoons butter

½ cup diced onion

4 tablespoons all-purpose flour

1 garlic clove, pressed

½ teaspoon dry mustard

¼ teaspoon cayenne pepper

½ teaspoon salt

½ teaspoon black pepper

2 cups fat-free milk

2 cups cooked jasmine white rice

12 ounces of frozen broccoli, carrots, and cauliflower (California mix)

2 cups diced, cooked chicken

1 cup shredded cheddar cheese

Directions

1. Preheat the oven to 350 degrees. In a large oven-safe skillet over medium heat, melt butter. Add onion and cook untilsoftened, about 2-3 minutes. Stir in flour and let it cook for 1 minute. Add garlic, dry mustard, cayenne pepper, salt, and black pepper. Stir in milk and let the sauce bubble and thicken, approximately 2-3 minutes.

2. Add cooked rice, vegetables, and chicken. Stir to coat. Sprinkle it with cheese. Place the skillet into the oven and bake for 30 minutes or until bubbling. Top with French fried onions for the last five minutes of cooking, if using.

Optional:

French fried onions as a topping

Nutrition Facts	Amount/serving	% Daily Value*	Amount/serving	% Daily Value*	
	Total Fat 20.0g	30%	Total Carbohydrates 41g	13%	* The percent Daily Value (DV) tells you how much a nutrient in a serving of food contributes to a daily diet. 2,000 calories a day is used for general nutrition advice.
4 servings	Saturated Fat 10.8g	54%	Dietary Fiber 5g	19%	
	Trans Fat 0.0g		Total Sugars 10g		
Calories 518 per serving	Cholesterol 51mg	17%			
	Sodium 602mg	26%	Protein 52g		
	Vitamin D 0mcg 0% · Calcium 213mg 21% · Iron 1mg 6% · Potassium 301mg 6%				

Taco Bubble Casserole

PREP TIME: 10 MIN   COOK TIME: 28 MIN   TOTAL TIME: 38 MIN

SERVINGS: 8

It's taco night in the form of a casserole! You may be surprised at how good this recipe is. It features black beans as well to boost fiber, and you can top it just like you would a taco!

Ingredients

1 pound lean ground beef

1 (15 ounce) can reduced-sodium black beans, drained and rinsed

1 (10 ounce) reduced-sodium tomato soup

¾ cup water

1 (1.25 ounce) envelope reduced-sodium taco seasoning

1 (12 ounce) can refrigerated buttermilk biscuits

2 cups shredded cheddar cheese

Toppings:

Shredded lettuce, diced tomatoes, salsa, nonfat plain Greek yogurt, guacamole, and green onions

Directions

1. Preheat the oven to 375 degrees. In a 12-inch oven-safe, non-stick skillet, cook beef over medium heat until no longer pink or it reaches a temperature of 160 degrees. Add black beans, soup, seasoning, and water.
2. Meanwhile, cut each biscuit into 8 pieces. Remove pan from the heat. Stir in biscuit pieces to coat.
3. Transfer pan to oven and bake for 20 minutes or until biscuits are golden brown. Sprinkle with cheese and bake for another 8 minutes. Serve with toppings and snacking vegetables.

Nutrition Facts	Amount/serving	% Daily Value*	Amount/serving	% Daily Value*	
	Total Fat 20.9g	32%	**Total Carbohydrates** 37g	12%	* The percent Daily Value (DV) tells you how much a nutrient in a serving of food contributes to a daily diet. 2,000 calories a day is used for general nutrition advice.
8 servings	Saturated Fat 9.0g	44%	Dietary Fiber 6g	23%	
	Trans Fat 0.7g		Total Sugars 5g		
Calories **448** per serving	**Cholesterol** 69mg	22%			
	Sodium 709mg	30%	**Protein** 28g		
	Vitamin D 0mcg 0% · Calcium 187mg 18% · Iron 4mg 22% · Potassium 466mg 9%				

Creamy Turkey and Noodles

PREP TIME: 13 MIN   COOK TIME: 30 MIN   TOTAL TIME: 33 MIN

SERVINGS: 6

This recipe is easy to make and you can even use chicken instead of turkey if you would like. Whenever I make this casserole, my family likes to eat a piece of whole wheat bread with it, either with a spreadable light butter or jam.

Ingredients

2 tablespoons butter

½ yellow onion, diced

3 tablespoons all-purpose flour

8 ounces of mixed frozen vegetables (corn, green beans, carrots, peas)

8 ounces of dry wide egg noodles

16 ounces of reduced-sodium chicken broth

1 cup milk

8 ounces of cooked, diced turkey or chicken

1 (10.75 ounce) can reduced-sodium cream of chicken soup

½ cup plain, nonfat Greek yogurt

4 ounces shredded cheddar cheese

Directions

1. Preheat the oven to 350 degrees. Melt butter in Dutch Oven or large, deep skillet on medium heat. Add onions and cook and stir for 3 minutes, or until crisp-tender. Sprinkle onions with flour. Add vegetables, dry pasta, 16 ounces of chicken broth, and milk. Cook over medium heat for 8–10 minutes or until noodles are tender.

2. Add turkey, soup, and Greek yogurt and gradually stir together until mixture is evenly coated. Top with cheese and cover. Bake for 30 minutes. During the last 10 minutes, remove the cover. Serve with whole wheat bread and snacking vegetables.

Nutrition Facts	Amount/serving	% Daily Value*	Amount/serving	% Daily Value*	
	Total Fat 10.0g	15%	**Total Carbohydrates** 44g	14%	* The percent Daily Value (DV) tells you how much a nutrient in a serving of food contributes to a daily diet. 2,000 calories a day is used for general nutrition advice.
6 servings	Saturated Fat 4.5g	22%	Dietary Fiber 3g	13%	
	Trans Fat 0.0g		Total Sugars 5g		
Calories 380	**Cholesterol** 84g	27%			
per serving	**Sodium** 512g	22%	**Protein** 29g		
	Vitamin D 0g 1% · Calcium 191g 19% · Iron 1g 7% · Potassium 531g 11%				

Sheet Pan Dinners

PREP TIME: 20 MIN   COOK TIME: 30 MIN   TOTAL TIME: 50 MIN   SERVINGS: 4

This recipe is easy to make and you can even use chicken instead of turkey if you would like. Whenever I make this casserole, my family likes to eat a piece of whole wheat bread with it, either with a spreadable light butter or jam.

Ingredients

Type of Protein	Vegetables	Seasonings
4 Chicken Breasts or Thighs — Bone In or Out	2 cups: Onion, red pepper, mushrooms, potatoes	1-2 tablespoons olive oil, 1-2 tablespoons Greek seasoning 1 tablespoon freshly squeezed lemon juice
4 Salmon Fillets	2 cups: Zucchini, onion, potatoes	1-2 tablespoons pesto sauce, 1 tablespoon olive oil ½ teaspoon combined salt and pepper 1 teaspoon freshly squeezed lemon juice or lemon zest
4 Pork Chops — Bone In or Out (one inch thick)	2 cups: Onion, red pepper, red potatoes	1-2 tablespoons olive oil ½ teaspoon combined salt and black pepper ½ teaspoon garlic powder ½ teaspoon dried rosemary

Directions

1. Pick a protein selection and the coordinating vegetables and seasonings.
2. Whisk together the seasonings in desired amounts in a large bowl. Toss in vegetables and protein and evenly coat.
3. On a sheet pan, spread out the protein and vegetables.
4. Bake at 450 degrees for 15-30 minutes, depending on the thickness of the protein, until proteins reach the following temperatures:
   a. Chicken: 165 degrees
   b. Fish: 145 degrees
   c. Pork: 145 degrees

Nutrition Facts	Amount/serving	% Daily Value*	Amount/serving	% Daily Value*	
	Total Fat 4.5g	6%	Total Carbohydrates 8g	2%	* The percent Daily Value (DV) tells you how much a nutrient in a serving of food contributes to a daily diet. 2,000 calories a day is used for general nutrition advice.
4 servings	Saturated Fat 0.5g	2%	Dietary Fiber 2g	9%	
	Trans Fat 0.0g		Total Sugars 2g		
	Cholesterol 0mg	0%			
Calories **190**	Sodium 83mg	3%	Protein 37g		
per serving					
	Vitamin D 0mcg 0% · Calcium 18mg 1% · Iron 1mg 3% · Potassium 149mg 3%				

*Nutrition facts based on chicken breasts with vegetables sheet pan meal.

Simple Side Dish:
Snacking Vegetable Platter

To balance out the meal, make a quick snacking vegetable platter.
This works great for family members that are already hungry, and it also
completes the meal!

Pick 2-3 vegetables for a platter, ½ cup per person:	**Pick your dip:**
Cucumber slices Celery sticks Carrot sticks Cherry tomatoes Sliced radishes Broccoli florets Cauliflower florets Bell pepper slices	1 cup plain nonfat Greek yogurt and ½ cup low fat mayonnaise, plus 3 tablespoons all purpose dill seasoning or 3 tablespoons Southwest seasoning or 3 tablespoons French onion seasoning

Which five recipes are you going to include on your menu map?

List them here:

1.

2.

3.

4.

5.

Did you add those recipes to your menu map as well? Be sure to do that before you move on to the last menu option of the week — pizza night! You now have four nights of meals done for the next month or more. What will you do with all this newfound time you will have? Keep reading, as we are almost done with the entire week, and then we will wrap things up with a challenge.

Resources on my website:

- Find the specific pots I recommend with how-to videos.
- Watch me cook in my recipe videos where I share how to get started with one-pot meals.
- Other helpful tools I recommend.

CHAPTER SEVEN

Pizza Recipes

Sometimes you don't know the value of a moment until it becomes a memory.

~Dr. Seuss

You have made it to the final step — family pizza night. In the last four chapters, you have made your list of meals to incorporate into your menu map to begin pressure cooking, air frying, smart grilling, and making one pot meals and sheet pan suppers. You are planning and going to cook with intention. I'm guessing it feels pretty good to have this process almost finished! We just have one night left. So let's finish strong!

When I was growing up, we had a family pizza night tradition on Friday nights. That meant homemade pizza and soda and sometimes a movie. My mom would make homemade crust on the pull out cutting board that was hidden beneath the old farmhouse counter. She would roll out the dough, add homemade pizza sauce she had canned from the garden, and then top it with vegetables, meats, and cheeses. I still remember the smell of it baking in the oven. That was the only night we could eat in the living room, where we would watch a movie together. It was a simple tradition that left long-lasting memories for me, so much so that I started a family pizza night tradition in our house too when the kids were young.

Of course, sometimes with my busy schedule working and picking up the kids, making homemade pizza just felt like too much. Pizza night became frozen pizza night during the times when I felt overwhelmed but wanted to continue the tradition. But I really craved the soft and chewy crusts just like I had growing up, so I started experimenting with making my own homemade crusts. You will find my five-minute pizza dough coming up in this chapter, along with my pressure cooker pizza dough too, since I use both of them regularly depending on how much time I have.

There are a few tools I think are essential when making pizza, and the top one is a pizza stone. A well-made pizza stone can be preheated in the oven, giving you the opportunity to slide the pizza onto it using a pizza peel and hear the crust start to sizzle. This allows it to become crispy on the outside and chewy on the inside. I also love that pizza stones keep pizza warm long after the pizza has been removed from the oven.

I believe every family needs a tradition because it is something they can count on during the chaos of the week. Even when everyone seems to be going in different directions, designating one night a week as family night to share pizza and a movie or pizza and game night can be a powerful way to connect with your family.

Other helpful tools in this chapter include:

- Pizza Stone
- Pizza Peel
- Pizza Cutter
- Baker's Roller
- Pastry Mat
- Pressure Cooker
- Manual Food Processor (for chopping and dicing vegetables)

Pizza night can also be customizable — meaning everyone can make and top their own pizza. Here are a list of toppings to consider:

Pizza Pie Making Chart:

Vegetables:	Meats:
<ul><li>Onions</li><li>Peppers</li><li>Mushrooms</li><li>Tomatoes</li><li>Zucchini</li><li>Carrots</li><li>Broccoli</li><li>Cauliflower</li><li>Pineapple</li></ul>	<ul><li>Turkey pepperoni</li><li>Turkey sausage crumbles</li><li>Ham</li><li>Canadian Bacon</li><li>Chicken</li><li>Ground Beef</li><li>Pork sausage</li><li>Traditional pepperoni — look for lower fat/lower sodium varieties</li></ul>
Cheeses:	Sauces:
<ul><li>Mozzarella</li><li>Parmesan</li><li>Muenster</li><li>Cheddar</li><li>Monterey Jack</li><li>Colby Jack</li></ul>	<ul><li>Pizza sauce</li><li>Barbecue sauce</li><li>Thai Peanut Sauce</li><li>Pesto Sauce</li><li>Taco Sauce</li><li>Enchilada Sauce</li></ul>

If you want to come up with your own pizza style, go for it! It can even be a great way to use up leftovers. You can simply pick a couple of vegetables, a meat/protein (or no meat at all), a sauce, and cheese for a creative way to get the family into the kitchen.

I have lots of pizza recipes for you to choose from in this chapter that I hope will match your tastes. Be sure to list out which ones you want to try at the end of the chapter!

Make Ahead Homemade Pizza Dough

PREP TIME: 68 MIN   COOK TIME: 10 MIN   TOTAL TIME: 78 MIN

MAKES ONE PIZZA CRUST

This dough is so easy to make. You can make it ahead of time or make it in the evening if you plan to have pizza that night. Using a pressure cooker to proof the dough makes it come together in half the normal time.

Ingredients

1 ¾ cups all purpose flour

1 ½ teaspoons instant yeast

1 teaspoon sugar

1 teaspoon salt

3/4 cup warm water (120–130 degrees Fahrenheit)

1 tablespoon olive oil

Directions

1. Combine all dry ingredients together. Add the warm water and olive oil. Mix until combined. If too dry, you can add an additional teaspoon of warm water.
2. Transfer onto a lightly floured pastry mat and gently knead until it forms a smooth, firm ball, about 5–6 minutes.
3. Brush the bottom of the pressure cooking pot with olive oil, add the dough, and brush oil on the top of the dough to lightly coat.
4. Put on the lid and set the pressure cooker to the "proof" setting. Adjust time to one hour. Alternatively, without a pressure cooker, place the dough in a warm, draft-free place in your kitchen to rise for two hours. If using this method, cover the dough with plastic wrap sprayed with nonstick cooking spray.
5. When you are ready to make pizza, place dough on lightly floured pastry mat and flatten with your hands, then roll with a rolling pin into a 12-inch circle

Nutrition Facts	Amount/serving	% Daily Value*	Amount/serving	% Daily Value*	
4 servings	Total Fat 3.5g	5%	Total Carbohydrates 8g	2%	* The percent Daily Value (DV) tells you how much a nutrient in a serving of food contributes to a daily diet. 2,000 calories a day is used for general nutrition advice.
	Saturated Fat 0.5g	2%	Dietary Fiber 0g	1%	
	Trans Fat 0.0g		Total Sugars 1g		
Calories 73 per serving	Cholesterol 0mg	0%			
	Sodium 561mg	24%	Protein 2g		
	Vitamin D 0mcg 0% · Calcium 1mg 0% · Iron 0mg 0% · Potassium 24mg 0%				

5-Minute Homemade Pizza Dough

PREP TIME: 5 MIN   COOK TIME: 10 MIN   TOTAL TIME: 15 MIN

MAKES ONE PIZZA CRUST

On nights when you don't have an hour to proof the dough, use this 5-minute recipe instead! It's fast, easy, and delicious. Plus, no one will know that it only took 5 minutes.

Ingredients

1 ¼ cups self-rising flour

¼ teaspoon baking soda

1 cup plain, low-fat Greek yogurt

Additional flour as needed

Directions

1. In a large bowl, combine dry ingredients; mix well. Stir in yogurt until combined. The mixture will look dry.
2. Turn dough out onto a lightly floured surface. Knead dough 4 minutes, sprinkling with additional self-rising flour as needed. When you are ready to make pizza, place dough on lightly floured pastry mat and flatten with your hands, then roll with a rolling pin into a 12-inch circle.

Nutrition Facts	Amount/serving	% Daily Value*	Amount/serving	% Daily Value*	
4 servings	**Total Fat** 0.5g	0%	**Total Carbohydrates** 37g	12%	* The percent Daily Value (DV) tells you how much a nutrient in a serving of food contributes to a daily diet. 2,000 calories a day is used for general nutrition advice.
	Saturated Fat 0.1g	0%	Dietary Fiber 1g	5%	
	Trans Fat 0.0g		Total Sugars 2g		
Calories 196 per serving	**Cholesterol** 3mg	0%			
	Sodium 659mg	28%	**Protein** 10g		
	Vitamin D 0mcg 0% · Calcium 221mg 22% · Iron 2mg 12% · Potassium 138mg 2%				

Note: Some recipes call for "par-baking" which is cooking the dough partially before the toppings are added. Then it's put back in the oven to finish baking.

Barbecue Chicken Pizza

PREP TIME: 5 MIN   COOK TIME: 12-15 MIN   TOTAL TIME: 17-20 MIN

MAKES ONE PIZZA

When you have leftover cooked chicken, use it to make this pizza. It's a fresh take on barbecue chicken — don't leave off the cilantro, it really adds a lot to the flavor!

Ingredients

1 recipe homemade pizza dough

¾ cup barbecue sauce

2 cups diced, cooked chicken breasts

1 small red onion, thinly sliced

1 green bell pepper, diced

1 cup shredded monterey jack cheese

1 cup shredded cheddar cheese

1 teaspoon barbecue seasoning

Fresh cilantro, minced

Directions

1. Heat oven to 425 degrees. Roll out pizza dough onto a pizza stone. Top with barbecue sauce, chicken, onion, and pepper. Sprinkle it with cheese and barbecue seasoning.
2. Bake pizza for 12-15 minutes or until the cheese is golden brown.

Nutrition Facts	Amount/serving	% Daily Value*	Amount/serving	% Daily Value*	
4 servings	**Total Fat** 15.2g	23%	**Total Carbohydrates** 25g	8%	* The percent Daily Value (DV) tells you how much a nutrient in a serving of food contributes to a daily diet. 2,000 calories a day is used for general nutrition advice.
	Saturated Fat 7.6g	37%	Dietary Fiber 1g	4%	
	Trans Fat 0.0g		Total Sugars 19g		
Calories 395 per serving	**Cholesterol** 38mg	12%			
	Sodium 810mg	35%	**Protein** 47g		
	Vitamin D 0mcg 0% · Calcium 309mg 30% · Iron 300mg 1668% · Potassium 192mg 4%				

*Nutrition facts for toppings only. Add your choice of pizza crust nutrient facts to have the total nutrition.

Healthy Hawaiian Pizza

PREP TIME: 5 MIN   COOK TIME: 12-15 MIN   TOTAL TIME: 17-20 MIN

MAKES ONE PIZZA

You can't go wrong with this pizza because it combines a few vegetables along with sweet pineapple and ham. If you don't want to add meat, just leave it off and go with pineapple and vegetables. It works both ways.

Ingredients

1 recipe homemade pizza dough

¾ cup pizza sauce

1 cup diced, canned pineapple chunks (you can also use fresh)

1 small red onion, finely diced

1 green bell pepper, finely diced

½ cup diced ham or Canadian Bacon

2 cups shredded mozzarella cheese

1 teaspoon pizza seasoning or Italian seasoning

Optional toppings: finely minced jalapeno peppers, turkey bacon, or regular bacon bits

Directions

1. Heat oven to 425 degrees. Roll out pizza dough onto a pizza stone. Top with sauce, pineapple, onion, pepper, and ham. Sprinkle it with cheese and pizza seasoning.
2. Bake pizza for 12-15 minutes or until the cheese is golden brown. Top with optional toppings if desired.

Nutrition Facts	Amount/serving	% Daily Value*	Amount/serving	% Daily Value*	
	Total Fat 10.4g	16%	**Total Carbohydrates** 17g	5%	* The percent Daily Value (DV) tells you how much a nutrient in a serving of food contributes to a daily diet. 2,000 calories a day is used for general nutrition advice.
4 servings	Saturated Fat 6.2g	31%	Dietary Fiber 2g	8%	
	Trans Fat 0.0g		Total Sugars 10g		
Calories 243 per serving	**Cholesterol** 43mg	14%			
	Sodium 773mg	33%	**Protein** 20g		
	Vitamin D 0g 1% · Calcium 478mg 47% · Iron 301mg 1671% · Potassium 392mg 8%				

*Nutrition facts for toppings only. Add your choice of pizza crust nutrient facts to have the total nutrition.

Garden Fresh Pizza

PREP TIME: 5 MIN   COOK TIME: 16-20 MIN   TOTAL TIME: 21-25 MIN

MAKES ONE PIZZA

In the spring, we plant our garden with lots of vegetables, including the ones you will find in this recipe. This recipe is a little different in that there is no traditional pizza sauce. Instead, you will find cheese below the vegetables as a new twist.

Ingredients

1 recipe homemade pizza dough

1 tablespoon garlic flavored olive or canola oil

½ cup shredded parmesan cheese, divided

1 cup shredded mozzarella cheese, divided

1 cup shredded cheddar cheese, divided

1 teaspoon Italian seasoning

1 small yellow onion, diced

1 green bell pepper, diced

1 large tomato, diced

1 small zucchini, thinly sliced

½ cup diced fresh mushrooms

Directions

1. Heat oven to 425. Roll out pizza dough onto a pizza stone and brush with oil. Par-bake pizza crust for 4-5 minutes in the oven.
2. Meanwhile, mix cheese with Italian seasoning in a large bowl. Remove crust from oven and sprinkle evenly with half of the cheese mixture, onions, peppers, tomato, zucchini, and mushrooms. Sprinkle evenly with remaining cheese.
3. Finish baking pizza for another 8-12 minutes or until the cheeses are golden brown.

Nutrition Facts	Amount/serving	% Daily Value*	Amount/serving	% Daily Value*	
4 servings	**Total Fat** 15.2g	23%	**Total Carbohydrates** 10g	3%	* The percent Daily Value (DV) tells you how much a nutrient in a serving of food contributes to a daily diet. 2,000 calories a day is used for general nutrition advice.
	Saturated Fat 6.9g	34%	Dietary Fiber 2g	7%	
	Trans Fat 0.1g		Total Sugars 5g		
Calories **224** per serving	**Cholesterol** 33mg	11%			
	Sodium 294mg	12%	**Protein** 12g		
	Vitamin D 0mcg 1% · Calcium 327mg 32% · Iron 300mg 1668% · Potassium 277mg 5%				

*Nutrition facts for toppings only. Add your choice of pizza crust nutrient facts to have the total nutrition.

Italian Sausage Pesto Pizza

PREP TIME: 5 MIN   COOK TIME: 16-20 MIN   TOTAL TIME: 21-25 MIN

MAKES ONE PIZZA

Pesto is one of my favorite sauces for pizza; it adds a fresh basil flavor that is hard to beat! I really like the chicken sausage in this recipe too. It's lower in calories and fat and adds that Italian flair.

Ingredients

1 recipe homemade pizza dough

½ cup fresh pesto sauce

1 ½ cups diced, fully cooked Italian flavored chicken sausage links

2 roma tomatoes, diced

1 ½ cups shredded Mozzarella cheese

½ cup shredded Parmesan cheese

Directions

1. Heat oven to 425 degrees. Roll out pizza dough onto a pizza stone. Par-bake for 4 minutes. Top with pesto sauce, chicken, onion, and pepper. Sprinkle it with cheese and barbecue seasoning.
2. Finish baking pizza for 8-12 minutes or until the cheese is golden brown.

Nutrition Facts	Amount/serving	% Daily Value*	Amount/serving	% Daily Value*	
4 servings	Total Fat 22.2g	34%	Total Carbohydrates 5g	1%	* The percent Daily Value (DV) tells you how much a nutrient in a serving of food contributes to a daily diet. 2,000 calories a day is used for general nutrition advice.
	Saturated Fat 9.7g	48%	Dietary Fiber 1g	2%	
	Trans Fat 0.3g		Total Sugars 3g		
Calories 317 per serving	Cholesterol 82mg	27%			
	Sodium 829mg	36%	Protein 23g		
	Vitamin D 0mcg 1% · Calcium 431mg 43% · Iron 0mg 1% · Potassium 89mg 1%				

*Nutrition facts for toppings only. Add your choice of pizza crust nutrient facts to have the total nutrition.

Taco Pizza

PREP TIME: 5 MIN   COOK TIME: 16-20 MIN   TOTAL TIME: 21-25 MIN

MAKES ONE PIZZA

Another taco night favorite — so easy and so good. The toppings make it all come together — don't leave them off. If your family likes tacos, they will love this pizza.

Ingredients

1 recipe homemade pizza dough

¾ cup salsa

1 (16 ounce) can refried beans

1 pound fully cooked ground beef, warmed

2 tablespoons reduced-sodium taco seasoning or Southwest seasoning

1-2 tablespoons water, as needed

1 ½ cups shredded cheddar cheese

Toppings:

1 ½ cups thinly shredded Romaine lettuce

2 roma tomatoes, diced

½ cup tortilla strips

Optional: olives, jalapeno peppers, additional taco sauce, non-fat plain Greek yogurt (in place of sour cream)

Directions

1. Heat oven to 425 degrees. Roll out pizza dough onto a pizza stone. Par-bake for 4 minutes. Mix salsa and refried beans together and spread evenly over the crust. Season cooked beef with taco seasoning, adding 1-2 tablespoons of water if necessary. Add beef mixture to pizza. Top with cheese.

2. Finish baking pizza for 8-12 minutes or until the cheese is golden brown. After cooking, top with additional toppings of lettuce, tomatoes, tortilla strips, and optional toppings as desired.

Nutrition Facts	Amount/serving	% Daily Value*	Amount/serving	% Daily Value*	
4 servings	**Total Fat** 19.0g	29%	**Total Carbohydrates** 39g	12%	* The percent Daily Value (DV) tells you how much a nutrient in a serving of food contributes to a daily diet. 2,000 calories a day is used for general nutrition advice.
	Saturated Fat 9.1g	45%	Dietary Fiber 8g	30%	
	Trans Fat 0.0g		Total Sugars 3g		
Calories per serving **408**	**Cholesterol** 33mg	11%			
	Sodium 1001mg	43%	**Protein** 18g		
	Vitamin D 0mcg 0% · Calcium 310mg 30% · Iron 4mg 22% · Potassium 595mg 12%				

*Nutrition facts for toppings only. Add your choice of pizza crust nutrient facts to have the total nutrition.

Chicken Fajita Pizza

PREP TIME: 5 MIN   COOK TIME: 16-20 MIN   TOTAL TIME: 21-25 MIN

MAKES ONE PIZZA

This pizza uses taco sauce as a base and then you top with all those traditional ingredients you would find in a chicken fajita. The fresh cilantro brings it all together. Be sure to add the toppings!

Ingredients

1 recipe homemade pizza dough

¾ cup medium taco sauce

2 cups diced, fully cooked chicken breasts

1-2 tablespoons chipotle rub or reduced-sodium fajita seasoning

1 bell pepper, thinly sliced

1 medium onion, thinly sliced

1 jalapeno pepper, finely diced

2 cups shredded cheddar cheese

Fresh cilantro, minced

Toppings: guacamole, lime, salsa, plain, non-fat Greek yogurt, halved cherry tomatoes

Directions

1. Heat oven to 425 degrees. Roll out pizza dough onto a pizza stone. Par-bake for 4-5 minutes. Top with taco sauce. Season chicken with chipotle rub and add chicken mixture to the pizza. Top evenly with bell pepper, onion, and jalapeno peppers. Sprinkle it with cheese.
2. Finish baking pizza for 8-12 minutes or until the cheese is golden brown. Top with fresh cilantro and additional toppings as desired.

Nutrition Facts		Amount/serving	% Daily Value*	Amount/serving	% Daily Value*	
		Total Fat 14.3g	22%	**Total Carbohydrates** 8g	2%	* The percent Daily Value (DV) tells you how much a nutrient in a serving of food contributes to a daily diet. 2,000 calories a day is used for general nutrition advice.
4 servings		Saturated Fat 7.6g	37%	Dietary Fiber 1g	4%	
		Trans Fat 0.0g		Total Sugars 2g		
		Cholesterol 38mg	12%			
Calories	**248**	**Sodium** 530mg	23%	**Protein** 29g		
per serving						
		Vitamin D 0mcg 0% · Calcium 296mg 29% · Iron 300mg 1666% · Potassium 101mg 2%				

*Nutrition facts for toppings only. Add your choice of pizza crust nutrient facts to have the total nutrition.

Detroit-Style Pizza

PREP TIME: 5 MIN   COOK TIME: 16-20 MIN   TOTAL TIME: 21-25 MIN

MAKES ONE PIZZA

This recipe may seem backwards because the sauce goes on last, but I can assure you, this is the best way to make this recipe. You will need a cast iron skillet for this recipe because you start the crust cooking process on the stovetop and finish it in the oven.

Ingredients

½ tablespoon canola oil

1 recipe homemade pizza dough

½ teaspoon Italian seasoning, divided

1 cup shredded Muenster cheese

1 cup shredded Mozzarella cheese

½ cup turkey sausage crumbles (fully cooked)

⅓ cup pizza sauce, plus more for additional topping if desired

Directions

1. Heat oven to 500 degrees. Brush a 12-inch cast iron skillet with canola oil. Roll out pizza dough into a 10-inch square and transfer the dough to the skillet, pressing dough up the sides. Pierce dough thoroughly with a fork. Sprinkle with ¼ teaspoon Italian seasoning. Place the skillet on the stove-top and cook over high heat for 2-3 minutes until the dough slightly puffs.

2. Remove pan from heat and top with cheeses all the way to the edges of the crust. Add the sausage crumbles and the remaining Italian seasoning. Dollop pizza sauce around the top of the pizza.

3. Bake pizza for 12-15 minutes or until the cheese is golden brown on the bottom rack of the oven. Serve with additional warmed pizza sauce if desired.

Nutrition Facts	Amount/serving	% Daily Value*	Amount/serving	% Daily Value*	
	Total Fat 16.5g	25%	Total Carbohydrates 4g	1%	* The percent Daily Value (DV) tells you how much a nutrient in a serving of food contributes to a daily diet. 2,000 calories a day is used for general nutrition advice.
4 servings	Saturated Fat 8.9g	44%	Dietary Fiber 0g	1%	
	Trans Fat 0.1g		Total Sugars 2g		
	Cholesterol 41mg	13%			
Calories 229 per serving	Sodium 556mg	24%	Protein 16g		
	Vitamin D 0mcg 2% · Calcium 368mg 36% · Iron 1mg 4% · Potassium 188mg 3%				

*Nutrition facts for toppings only. Add your choice of pizza crust nutrient facts to have the total nutrition.

Thai Chicken Pizza

PREP TIME: 5 MIN   COOK TIME: 12-15 MIN   TOTAL TIME: 17-20 MIN

MAKES ONE PIZZA

Ingredients

1 recipe homemade pizza dough or 2 naan crusts

½ cup sweet Thai chili sauce

1 carrot, grated

1 medium zucchini, grated

1 red bell pepper, diced

½ cup canned diced pineapple

2 cups diced, fully cooked chicken breasts

1-½ cups shredded mozzarella cheese

2 green onions, thinly sliced

¼ cup fresh cilantro, minced

Directions

1. Heat oven to 425 degrees. Roll out pizza dough onto a pizza stone. Par-bake for 7 minutes. Top with sweet Thai chili sauce, grated carrots, zucchini, pepper, pineapple, and chicken. Sprinkle it with cheese.
2. Bake pizza for 12-15 minutes or until the cheese is golden brown. Sprinkle with green onions and cilantro.

Nutrition Facts	Amount/serving	% Daily Value*	Amount/serving	% Daily Value*	
	Total Fat 7.2g	11%	Total Carbohydrates 36g	11%	* The percent Daily Value (DV) tells you how much a nutrient in a serving of food contributes to a daily diet. 2,000 calories a day is used for general nutrition advice.
4 servings	Saturated Fat 3.7g	18%	Dietary Fiber 2g	9%	
	Trans Fat 0.2g		Total Sugars 12g		
Calories **296** per serving	Cholesterol 21mg	6%			
	Sodium 776mg	33%	Protein 27g		
	Vitamin D 0mcg 1% · Calcium 248mg 24% · Iron 300mg 1668% · Potassium 327mg 6%				

*Nutrition facts for toppings only. Add your choice of pizza crust nutrient facts to have the total nutrition.

Simple Side Dish: Fresh Fruit and Dips

Rounding out any pizza meal with fruit is a great way to boost nutrition.
Mix and match your favorite fruits so you have some variety.
And try the dip, it's delicious!

Pick a fruit, **planning for ½ cup per person:** Strawberries Grapes Apples Oranges Pineapple Pears Blueberries Raspberries Bananas	**Mix together:** 8 oz your favorite Greek yogurt flavor plus 8 oz whipped topping

Which five recipes are you going to include on your menu map?

List them here:

1.

2.

3.

4.

5.

Can you believe that with this chapter, you now have all the recipes you need for your Forever Dinner Plan? Add the recipes you chose in each chapter to your menu map, and let the meal making begin. Don't forget to download the bonus menu map workbook so you have the shopping lists to go with each day of the week.

This strategy is so easy and so doable, will save you so much time in the kitchen now, and will give you more time with your family in the long run. Now turn the page for an easy challenge to help you really make it happen.

Resources on my website:

- Find the specific pizza stone I recommend with how-to videos.
- Watch me cook in my recipe videos where I share how to get started with a weekly pizza night.
- Other helpful tools I recommend.

CHAPTER EIGHT

Next Steps

Cooking is love made visible.

~Unknown

The Forever Dinner Plan — does it feel like a forever dinner plan? In this case, forever means you can rely on this one simple meal plan for your busiest season as a mom – when the kids are in all the activities and you are running from one thing to the next, when there are work meetings that last into the evening, and when you are tired of making decisions all day long and suffer from decision fatigue.

This is why I wrote this book. I've been in all of these places and I wish I would have had a plan like this for myself at that time. Instead, it took me years to develop this for myself and for you. Making the busiest night into pressure cooker night. Ensuring that we have a family pizza night along with a family movie night or game night every week. Spending time together around the kitchen table rather than overspending on restaurant meals that aren't as healthy. Saving your sanity and making healthier air fryer meals. Saving on clean up time with one-pot meals.

When I look back over my time as a mom with both kids in the house, it was my favorite time of my life. Now that my son is grown and off on his next adventure, the thing I miss most is the cooking I was able to do for all four of us, including the "thanks for making it" at the end of the meal and the messy dishes I would wash. I miss the empty pots and pans because the four of us ate all of the recipe, leaving little for leftovers. I miss the conversation at the table and the laughs and stories we shared together. And, of course, those smiles and hugs at the end of the day were and still are my favorite.

Because kids grow up, the frequency of all these things becomes less because they move on with their lives. So every time we are together I try to soak it all in. I treasure those times more now, but I wish I would have treasured them more then. Of course I still cook for the three of us, but it is different now — there are more leftovers. There always feels like "someone is missing" at the table. There are less helpers in the kitchen before and after the meal. It's different.

I wrote this book so you can cherish those small moments with your family now and stop worrying about what's for dinner every day. So you can stop scavenging through all the cookbooks, the websites, and the magazines (not that they aren't fun to look at), and really just cook with joy in your heart. I want you to do your very best to treasure all the moments because, as they say, "the days are long but the years are short."

So it's time for a challenge — a five-dinner challenge. Pick one tool featured in this book (meaning pick one chapter from this book), and use that specific tool and make five recipes in that chapter to make dinner for five nights.

When you pick one tool and make those five dinners, you will gain:

- Confidence in using that tool simply by using it every day
- New recipes that are so family-friendly that your family will love them
- A new sense of confidence in yourself in pulling a meal together that you can be proud of because the planning is done for you
- Joy in your kitchen that will transfer to joy within your family
- Find the 5 Dinner Challenge here: www.jenhaugen.com

To help you with this challenge, simply go to my website where I have an exclusive bonus for you. You can pick the chapter you want, and find the full shopping list for all of those recipes in one spot. Then all you need to do is take that list to your kitchen, circle the items you need, and tell your smart kitchen friend "Alexa" or "Google Home" to put those items on the shopping list. You can then head to the store with an organized list, or order your groceries to be delivered. During my recipe testing for this book, I used this exact same method and I was in and out of the grocery store in thirty minutes.

- Download the Dinner, Done! Planner for free which includes a printable menu map just for you, a bonus six-week, done-for-you menu, essential pantry, refrigerator and freezer lists plus the kitchen tools I recommend. You can find it that here: www.jenhaugen.com/dinnerdone

On top of those exclusive resources for you, here are some other ways we can work together:

- Personal culinary coaching and virtual cooking classes.
    - Visit jenhaugen.com and click the services page for more information.
- Follow me and connect with me on my Facebook Page @JenHaugenRD and Instagram @JenHaugenRD.

As you finish this book, take a moment to reflect on what has been the most powerful tool for you that you are going to implement right now. What are the top three things you are going to change or do in order to move forward with the Forever Dinner Plan?

1.

2.

3.

Share these with me by emailing jen@jenhaugen.com - I would love to hear your next steps on your journey to your Forever Dinner Plan, or even see a picture of your menu map. I can't wait to hear from you. Dinner is done!

Recipe Name:

_____

CIRCLE THE COOKING STYLE:

PRESSURE COOKING   AIR FRYING   SMART GRILL   ONE-POT   PIZZA

PREP TIME: _____   COOK TIME: _____.   TOTAL TIME: _____

SERVES: _____

Ingredients   Directions

Recipe Name:

_____

CIRCLE THE COOKING STYLE:

PRESSURE COOKING   AIR FRYING   SMART GRILL   ONE-POT   PIZZA

PREP TIME: _____   COOK TIME: _____.   TOTAL TIME: _____

SERVES: _____

Ingredients   Directions

Recipe Name:

_____

CIRCLE THE COOKING STYLE:

PRESSURE COOKING   AIR FRYING   SMART GRILL   ONE-POT   PIZZA

PREP TIME: _____   COOK TIME: _____.   TOTAL TIME: _____

SERVES: _____

Ingredients   ## Directions

Recipe Name:

_____

CIRCLE THE COOKING STYLE:

PRESSURE COOKING   AIR FRYING   SMART GRILL   ONE-POT   PIZZA

PREP TIME: _____   COOK TIME: _____.   TOTAL TIME: _____

SERVES: _____

Ingredients   ## Directions

Recipe Name:

_____

CIRCLE THE COOKING STYLE:

PRESSURE COOKING   AIR FRYING   SMART GRILL   ONE-POT   PIZZA

PREP TIME: _____   COOK TIME: _____.   TOTAL TIME: _____

SERVES: _____

Ingredients   ## Directions

Acknowledgments

I want to thank my family, who inspired this book with the treasured times we have spent in the kitchen together. The laughs, the smiles, and even the arguments will never be forgotten, as they filled my heart with joy each and every time. Because with those, I knew that I had a family to love and a family who loved me.

To Riley, my dear son — your constant appreciation for my cooking brought joy to me each and every day. I love how you always looked forward to my meals, and when you say how much you miss them, it warms my heart. Your determination and helpful and caring nature have always inspired me.

To Emma, my dear daughter — your helpfulness in the kitchen made cooking and cleaning up a lot more fun. I treasure our times standing at the kitchen sink together with the stories and lessons we shared. I love your enthusiasm for being in the kitchen to create recipes for others too. Your decisiveness, strong beliefs, and leadership skills have always inspired me.

To my husband, who at the heart of my life is my rock of steadiness, playfulness, and joy — I love looking across the kitchen table at you and being grateful for the family and life we have created together. (All because I took a chance and asked you on our first of many dates.)

Read More

Craving more? Check out *The Mom's Guide to a Nourishing Garden.*

Written for the mom who craves simplicity and balance back in her life, this book is about how a family vegetable garden can not only grow healthy food that nourishes our families, but also nourishes our souls. Using the idea of a "compost" recipe to create a more nourishing life as a mom, the author, a registered dietitian and Certified Master Gardener, guides the reader through the idea of why gardening together as a family matters so much and how planting connections in the garden sprout into memories that last a lifetime.

Including everything you need to know to plant more than thirty-five different fruits and vegetables in the garden, along with thirty garden fresh recipes, this book makes family vegetable gardening not only achievable, but fun at the same time!

Author Bio

Jen Haugen, RDN, LD is an award-winning registered dietitian who has published two books, has a column with the Austin Daily Herald, and has executed over a thousand cooking segments on television and in her own kitchen. She has a degree in Dietetics as well as Food & Nutrition, and completed her year-long dietetic internship at the competitive Mayo Clinic in Rochester, MN. You can follow her on YouTube, Instagram and Facebook @jenhaugenRD. She is an independent kitchen consultant, and enjoys camping at state parks, growing herbs, vegetables, and flowers, and most of all, being with her family. And when she was feeling brave, she once applied to compete on Food Network star.

Would you write a review?

I would really appreciate your feedback on my book and would love to hear what you have to say. Perhaps you have an idea for my next book as well. Please leave me a helpful review on Amazon letting me know what you thought of the book and how it has helped you.

Every review matters, and you can "give back" just by sharing your feedback!

Thank you for taking a moment to help me with your review!

Made in the USA
Coppell, TX
28 March 2022

75660319R00079